SPEEDWAY PUBLIC LIBRARY

3 5550 43105 4215

W9-CAY-474

The Cayman Islands

917.292 PAL
Palmer, Jenny.
Cayman Islands

10/09

WITHDRAWN
Speedway Public Library

SPEEDWAY PUBLIC LIBRARY
SPEEDWAY, INDIANA

MACMILLAN

Macmillan Education
Between Towns Road, Oxford OX4 3PP
A division of Macmillan Publishers Limited
Companies and representatives throughout the world

ISBN: 978-1-4050-7725-5

Text and photography © Jenny Palmer 2009
Design and illustration © Macmillan Publishers Limited 2009

First published 2009

All rights reserved; no part of this publication may be
reproduced, stored in a retrieval system, transmitted in any
form, or by any means, electronic, mechanical, photocopying,
recording, or otherwise, without the prior written permission
of the publishers.

These materials may contain links for third party websites.
We have no control over, and are not responsible for, the
contents of such third party websites. Please use care when
accessing them.

Designed by Amanda Easter
Typeset by J & D Glover Ltd
Cover design by Gary Fielder at Conkas
Map by Peter Harper
Cover photographs by Jenny Palmer
Photographs on pages 98, 99 by Solomon Baksh

Dedication
For Joshua, Sophie and Nelson

Printed and bound in Malaysia

2013 2012 2011 2010 2009
10 9 8 7 6 5 4 3 2 1

Contents

Acknowledgements

Danielle Woolf at the Caribbean Club, Andreas and Natalie Ugland, Eliza Strachan, Barbara Levey and Ed Powers of the Book Nook, Dan Sydlowski at the Westin Casuarina, The Courtyard Marriott, Villas of the Galleon, Eldemire's Guest House, Avis Rentals, Donald McDougall at the Cayman Islands Department of Tourism, Joshua and Sophie Palmer and Nelson Ebanks.

Map

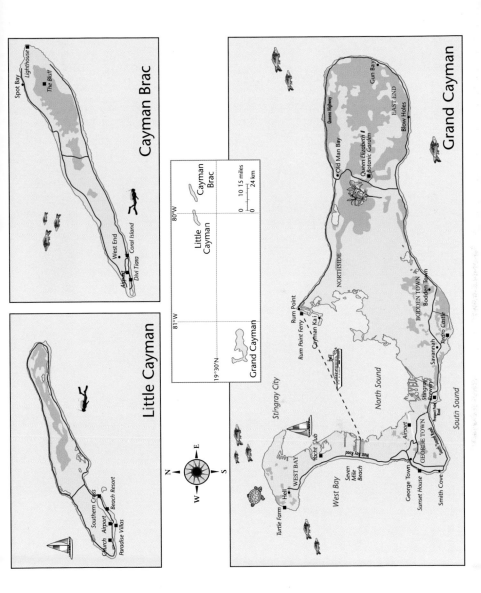

Cayman Brac

Spot Bay
Lighthouse
The Bluff

West End
Coral Island
Airport
Divi Tiara

Little Cayman

Southern Cross
Airport
Beach Resort
Church
Paradise Villas

N
W — E
S

81°W   80°W

19°30'N

Grand Cayman

Little Cayman

Cayman Brac

0   10 15 miles
0   24 km

Grand Cayman

Gun Bay
EAST END
Blow Holes
Queens Highway
Queen Elizabeth II
Botanic Garden
Old Man Bay
NORTHSIDE
BODDEN TOWN
Bodden Town
Pedro Castle
Savannah
Rum Point
Rum Point Ferry
Cayman Kai
North Sound
Stingray City
Stingray Brewery
Frank Sound Road
Airport
Hell Fer Road
WEST BAY
Yacht Club
West Bay
Seven Mile Beach
George Town
GEORGE TOWN
Sunset House
Smith Cove
Soto South Road
South Sound
Turtle Farm
Hell

▲ Drake, turtles and caimans on John Broad's 500-year mural in George Town

❶ History of the Cayman Islands

On Wednesday 10 May 1503, **Christopher Columbus** and his crew of 12 sailors were the first Europeans to record a sighting of the Cayman Brac and Little Cayman. Columbus called the islands 'Las Tortugas' as there were many turtles to be seen on and around them. By 1526, there were maps labelled Caymanos and in 1586, **Sir Francis Drake**, nicknamed El Draco (the Dragon) by the Spaniards, came across the islands when sailing on *HMS Bon Aventure* from Cartegna in Colombia. He was heading a convoy of 23 ships which had been on a retaliation mission against King Philip I, and the crews saw the native caimans (small crocodiles) which probably sealed the name for the Islands.

Another emissary of Queen Elizabeth I, **Martin Frobisher**, sailed in the same convoy and was Vice-Admiral on the *Primrose*. A member of his crew gave the following account of the islands:

'The 18 of Aprill wee set saile the seconde time from Carthagina and the xxij of Aprill we fell with and Ile that had no people in hit. There wee fownde strawnge kindes of beastes & killed more than xx Aligatos. Those bee such serpentes as have bin in London to be seene. There weare Crocadiles which did Incounter & fight with vs, they live bothe in the sea & on lande. We tooke divers & made verie good meate of them, some of the same weare ten foote in lenghte. Also wee killed other little beastes like cattes & other little serpentes abowte 2 foote longe called Guanos, with a greate number of Turtles of huge bignes which served vs for verie good meate. This Ilande is a verie Deserte & wildernesse & so full of woodes as hit can growe. Wee thought to have watered there but could finde none. Wee staid there ij Daies & set the woodes on fire & soe departed'.

In 1630, a Dutch warship called the *Dophijn* was wrecked at the Cayman Islands and the yacht built from the broken timbers was renamed the *Cayman*. The islands became stopping posts for the supply of fresh turtle meat, fresh water and for careening of vessels needing repair. And, as Michael Craton says in his book *Founded upon the Seas – A History of the Cayman Islands*, Captain Henry

Morgan knew the islands well and from 1664 to 1670, launched attacks on the Spanish from them.

Henry Morgan

Henry Morgan was born in Wales in 1635 and, as a young man of 20, left Portsmouth as part of the expedition to Hispaniola which took Jamaica from the Spanish. The fleet stopped off at Montserrat, Nevis and St Kitts (which had been a British Colony since 1623) and picked up large numbers of soldiers en route. The commanders in charge of the expedition were Penn and Venables under orders from Oliver Cromwell. They were defeated at Santo Domingo and Hispaniola (now the Dominican Republic and Haiti), so they tried their luck by attacking Jamaica instead. In all, 5000 of the original 7000 soldiers lost their lives on Hispaniola and Jamaica. Morgan survived, but had learnt lessons about attacking Spanish forts.

Thus Port Royal on the coast of Jamaica was taken by the English, although there were still some Spanish resistance fighters in the mountains that had to be controlled. At this time, the Jamaican town of Port Royal had 4500 residents and 1500 slaves. This made it bigger than New York. **Thomas Modyford** became the English Governor of Jamaica.

The Cayman Islands were similarly recognised to be under British control as a dependency of Jamaica. In 1659, **Christopher Mings** led privateers on an expedition against the Spanish Main taking and pillaging Campeche, Coro, Cumana and Puerto Cabello. He led another to Santiago in 1662.

Morgan became commander of his own ships and, for the next 30 years, his name was legendary for brave and daring attacks on the Spanish Empire. Many places, restaurants and bars and indeed rum bottles in Cayman bear his name today. Morgan gathered a group of adventurers, runaway slaves and ferocious pirates and made them into the most feared army in the Caribbean. There were many other pirates and buccaneers about in those waters and Morgan saw that the only answer was to fight fire with fire. He terrorised Spanish merchant ships and devastated cities – with his commission from Charles II he was a legal pirate. Morgan's last raid, an assault on Panama, helped break Spain's hold on the Americas.

Morgan learnt to give no quarter to the Spaniards and to become as ruthless and cruel as other very successful pirates. He had to cultivate a feared reputation to get the results he needed. Torturing captives was part of this. Tortures included woolding, which was to tie a knotted rope around a captive's head and turn it with a stick until the eyes popped out. Some were chained on their belly, while fire was applied to their head and feet, and starved while a loaf of bread lay just out of reach. The Spanish Inquisition's tortures were already legendary, so much was probably learned from them and used in retaliation. Many of the tortured would not give up details of the whereabouts of their silver until mutilated beyond recognition. Morgan killed anyone that didn't finally give information, but he hated being called a pirate – he regarded himself as a soldier of the English King.

Morgan raided Granada during the period 1663–65. He went on to raid Portobelo in 1668, Maracaibo in 1669 and Panama in 1670 and sailed very near to the Cayman Islands on his way to attack Granada in Honduras. He eventually returned to Port Royal a rich man.

Cayman was used as a rendezvous before the attacks on Portobelo and Marcaibo. **Manuael Rivero Pardal** used Cayman in a counter attack for the Spanish in 1669, which encouraged and justified Morgan's last raid on Panama in 1670. In 1672, Morgan was arrested and brought back to England while Charles II considered what to do about the peace treaty with Spain. Modyford, the Jamaican Governor during Morgan's raids, was put in the Tower of London for a couple of years to prove to the Spanish that the English wanted to follow the path of peace. But Charles II still wanted Jamaica, so he sent Morgan back as deputy governor because of his knowledge of the local pirates and to defend the Island, and eventually freed Modyford. In 1692, Port Royal was totally destroyed in an earthquake and settlers moved across the bay to what is now Kingston. Morgan's raids ensured that Jamaica, and hence the Cayman Islands, remained English.

Morgan must have visited Cayman several times, particularly for his men to gather turtle for voyages. His flagship, the 22-cannon *Satisfaction*, was discovered in the Cayman Islands where it was patrolling Spanish waters just before Morgan's raid on Panama and it was ordered back to Jamaica.

Morgan's adventures

Morgan had planned a raid on Cartegna with a ship called the *Oxford*, a 72-foot frigate armed with 26 guns and 125 men for the defence of his Majesty's plantation of Jamaica. A fleet of 12 ships and 900 men was to accompany the *Oxford* on its mission. He held a council of war aboard the *Oxford* and, once all the captains had officially decided that Cartegna was to be the destination, a punch bowl was filled and the party began. As was the tradition on such evenings, guns were fired under the tables and pistols shot into the sky. One of these gun-shots ignited the gunpowder on board the *Oxford* and it exploded, destroying the ship. Morgan and the other captains survived but 200 men were killed and the raid on Cartegna had to be called off.

Once, while trying to get out of a tricky situation, Morgan sent out a ship, covered with banners to make it look like his flagship, towards a Spanish fleet. This boat was actually empty – apart from wooden cut-out figures of pirates and their cutlasses – and the deck was covered with tar over palm leaves and logs to simulate cannons. When the Spanish shot at the ship heading straight for them, it burst into flames, setting fire to their own tinder-box of a ship with flammable sails, gunpowder in the hold and ropes covered in fat. Ships like this were called fireships.

Morgan made **Don Alonzo**, the Spanish leader, think he was being attacked on land by sending ashore canoes laden with men in full sight of the castle's look-outs. What they did not know was that Morgan's men did not disembark, but lay down in the bottom of the apparently empty canoes for the return journey. The sailors then climbed back onto their ship from the other side, unseen by the look-outs. All the Spanish cannons had been wheeled to the landward side to repel the expected attack and the seaside forts lay empty. At night, Morgan lifted anchor and the currents took them quietly out into the channel. Then they set sail and surprised the Spanish.

These are examples of the adventures that privateers were having around the Caribbean. The Cayman Islands would serve as a stopping-off post to refresh captains and their crews after battles.

PIRATES AND PRIVATEERS

There are many sources for the history of buccaneers and adventurers on the Cayman Islands. The main reason for the piracy on the waters

▲ A pirate

around the Caribbean Islands between 1500 and 1650 was that 180 tons of gold was reported to have flowed through the port of Seville (known as the Golden Doorway) and 16 000 tons of silver from the Potosi mine were discovered in Bolivia in 1544. All this made its way across the seas, and hijacking the boats carrying the treasure was a lucrative, though dangerous, business. The English wanted a share of this gold and silver, not to mention the Spanish colonies, and privateers were commissioned to carry out the work.

Privateering was different from pirating only because the commander of a privateer was travelling under a commission from the English Crown, which thus legalised their actions. Privateers had to share treasure with the nation licensing them. Pirates could keep all the treasure for themselves. Privateers were really just licensed pirates, but their behaviour and tactics were the same. Morgan learnt fast that the only way to win was to have a crew as bloodthirsty and as ruthless as the other pirate crews about. One of the pirates he learnt from, through tales of his ruthlessness was the Frenchman **D'Ollonais**.

Henry VIII had invented privateering in order to increase his income. Pirates, or buccaneers, were a mixture of escaped slaves, political refugees and adventure seekers. Sometimes, sailors who had started out from England on a merchant ship that had been captured by pirates would choose to join a band of desperate men to seek their fortune. It was a well-told tale that **John Ward**, an Englishman, had sailed to Algiers and assembled a pirate army that captured many ships loaded with spices and treasure and became very rich. Pirates were very frightening in appearance as many had missing eyes, arms or legs from constant battles. They wore treasure around their necks and a mixture of clothes captured from French and Spanish merchant ships – brightly coloured damasks and velvets. Any man who joined the pirates received an equal share of the captured treasure.

Buccaneers got their name from the people on Hispaniola in the 1600s who produced 'boucan' – smoked strips of beef which were traded with passing ships. They were a mixed race of Scots, Irish, Dutch, French, Caribbean and African. Their last names were not used, their first ones were normally invented and their pasts were not discussed. These men rejected the bourgeois life and survived on boucan, turtle and water. Their muskets were prized possessions, normally made by French gunsmiths and were essential for survival in battles. These muskets were very accurate, which gave the pirates a distinct advantage. The hammer might be shaped as a dolphin and, etched onto the sides, would be a picture of Jupiter or Mars throwing thunderbolts from the clouds. Every pirate carried a good musket and a pair of working pistols. Successful pirates dressed like an English gentleman with a damask waistcoat, breeches and a great deal of gold jewellery. At the beginning of an expedition it was the tradition to meet on the captain's flagship to reach a mutual decision about the next voyage over a bowl of rum punch.

There was a strong code of conduct and articles of piracy, which were drawn up and sworn on the Bible. Injured men were looked

▲ Young pirates swearing to abide by the code of conduct on the *Anne Bonny*

after and compensated for their bravery and wounds sustained during battle. The compensation for the loss of a right arm would be 600 pieces of eight, a left arm 500, a right leg 500, a left 400, an eye 100 and a finger 100. The first man to board an enemy ship or throw a grenade would receive extra pieces of eight – the gold coins which were currency at the time. Even though the code was sworn over a Bible, these buccaneers were individualists at heart and did not side with any particular religion. They were free to be employed by whoever gave them a commission, be it Catholic French or Spanish or the increasingly Protestant British. Pirates would hope to get gold and silver from a ship but the cargoes would also include animal skins, logwood, sugar and tortoiseshell, all of which were very valuable.

Once the buccaneers received their booty, they spent it ashore in a matter of days, even though they had suffered greatly in the process of gaining the treasure. Many dangers faced the men who went on such adventures – they could catch malaria from mosquitoes, be stung by scorpions, bitten by poisonous snakes or meet unfriendly Indians. Food was normally very scarce and, when the first stock had run out, they would have to eat anything that came their way. Life at sea and exploring unknown islands and mainland was far from being comfortable or safe, but, whenever they arrived back home, they would spend their takings and soon return to sea to earn some more.

Townspeople and traders in Port Royal liked the pirates because, when they were in town between raids, they had money to spend which helped businesses to flourish. They were feared, but at the same time seen as protectors – a kind of militia. The English found it better to have pirates as privateers on the side of the Crown than have them working for themselves. There was also the danger that, when they were left independent, they might receive commissions from the Portuguese or French.

After the Treaty of Utrecht in 1713, England was at peace with Spain and France and legitimate privateer activities in the Americas began to slow down. Nevertheless, younger sailors knew no other business and continued plundering vessels. In 1717, a proclamation was given offering the King's pardon to any pirate that surrendered at a certain time. Some took advantage of the pardon, but soon went back to their old ways, so piracy did not cease. There are countless pirate tales from the time after Henry Morgan, including one in Daniel Defoe's *General History of the Pyrates*, published in 1724, about the Welshman John Evans who left Port Royal in 1722.

SPEEDWAY PUBLIC LIBRARY
SPEEDWAY, INDIANA

Pirates

John Evans arrived in Grand Cayman aboard the Dutch ship *Lucretia* in 1723 after a great many adventures and plundering of Spanish, Dutch, New England and Jamaican vessels. He had been a mate on a merchant ship, but, dissatisfied with his wages, he and some of his shipmates decided to turn pirate. On the north coast of Jamaica they robbed houses and took over a small sloop with four cannons, renamed her the *Scourer* and sailed for Hispaniola. On their way, they captured a rich Spanish ship which yielded much treasure for each man on board, and gained more ships as they progressed. On approaching the Cayman Islands, the boatswain of the *Scourer* quarrelled with Evans and challenged him to a fight. Evans started to fight but the boatswain drew a pistol and shot him through the head, jumped overboard and swam to shore. The crew caught the boatswain and he was shot in the chest. Boatswain's Bay on Grand Cayman is named after this man. The main part of the treasure brought ashore probably included gold and silver coins, bars of gold, silver ingots, wine and brandy. Stories like this led to the many legends about buried treasure on the Islands.

Calico Jack Rackham was another famous pirate who gave his name to Calico Jack's bar on West Bay Beach and Rackham's pub on the waterfront in George Town. He took over New Providence in The Bahamas in the 1700s.

Edward Teach (or Thatch) – known as **Blackbeard** – was born in Bristol and served in a privateer vessel during the wars against Spain. In 1716 he took command of a captured French sloop with 40 guns which he renamed the *Queen Anne's Revenge*. He joined up with a Barbadian pirate, Major Stede Bonnet, on a 10-gun sloop called simply Revenge. Blackbeard got his name from the magnificent, very long beard which was said to cover most of his face. He plaited his beard and tied ribbons and coins in it. He carried many pistols and stuck a lighted match on each side of his hat to emphasise his fierce and wild appearance. Once he shot a shipmate in the knee by shooting under the table. Sometimes, he would kill one of his men so they would not forget his power and leadership. It is probably the pictures of Blackbeard that inspired Johnny Depp in the film *Pirates of the Caribbean* for his character Jack Sparrow.

Queen Anne's Revenge and *Revenge* both flew a black flag with a skull and cross bones and, after capturing and plundering several sloops in the Gulf of Honduras in 1717, they sailed for Grand Cayman to repair and refit the ships. Blackbeard continued his terrorising ways until 1718 when Lieutenant Maynard of *HMS Pearl* caught and killed him. Blackbeard's head was taken to Bath in North Carolina where his men were then tried and condemned to death.

Edward Low was an Englishman who became a pirate. He had started early in his life of crime, and had raised contributions from his classmates at school. He never learnt to read and write. He and his brother occupied themselves by pick-pocketing and housebreaking. It was said that the young Edward gamed with the footmen in the lobby at the House of Commons in London. Low joined the company of a sloop bound for Honduras to cut logwood. He commanded a small boat which ferried the woodcutters upriver, but he must have grown bored because, when ordered out for another cutting trip, Low took up a musket and fired at the captain. He missed, however, and shot another man through the head. The next day Low and his crew captured a small ship and declared themselves 'at war against all the world'.

They retreated to the Cayman Islands to plan more plundering voyages and it was here that he met and joined up with George Lowther.

George Lowther had been a mate on a vessel which had belonged to the Royal African Company under the name *Gambia Castle*. While waiting for cargo on the River Gambia, Lowther had angered the ship's captain who then ordered him to be punished. His fellow shipmates supported him and 'took up handspikes and threatened to knock down the first man to carry out the captain's order'. Lowther took control of the ship and he and the crew 'sought their fortunes upon the seas'. The *Gambia Castle* was renamed *Delivery* and set a course for the West Indies, flying the black flag. These were times when if things did not go your way you could, if brave enough, change their course and make your own fortune.

At West Bay on Grand Cayman, Lowther met up with Edward Low and the men joined forces to increase their chances of successful plundering. Low became second in command of *Delivery*. He was 'wanton in cruelties torturing men if their behaviour or look displeased hime'. He cut off one captain's ears, slit his nose and plundered his ship before letting it proceed. One day, in 1723, with another pirate named Harris, he chased and attacked a 20-gun man-of-war, *HMS Greyhound*. The *Greyhound*'s captain let them pursue him for two hours until he was ready for combat. When he was quite prepared, he tacked towards the pirates and waited until they came within a musket's shot before opening fire on the sloops. Harris' boat was destroyed but Low escaped in *Fancy*. Harris and his crew surrendered. A trial was held at Rhode Island and 25 men were executed.

Low continued and went on to capture a sloop which was whaling off the coast of Nantucket. The captain, stripped naked, was whipped and his ears were cut off before he was shot through the head. The sloop was plundered and sunk, while the crew were given a small boat with a small amount of food. In Newfoundland, Low took French vessels and manned them with pirates to raid nearby harbours but, during this voyage, died. Some say he was killed by his own men as a result of his cruel and tyrannical behaviour.

In September 1730, a Spanish 54-gun warship *Genoesa* was shipwrecked at the Pedro shoals, south of Jamaica. The boat had been carrying the Governor of Panama and a large amount of gold and silver coins and bars of gold and silver ingots. Three vessels were sent out to the rescue. One of them brought ashore 240 survivors but no treasure. *HMS Experiment* was sent to guard the wreck but, in the meantime, many sloops had been salvaging the treasure for themselves and they had escaped to the Cayman Islands before the *Experiment* appeared. *HMS Tryall* was sent out and brought in nearly 32 000 gold and silver coins, eight bars of gold and more than 100 silver ingots, but this was only a small fraction of what had been on board. Governor Hunter of Jamaica issued a proclamation against the captains of two of the original rescue boats, presuming them to have stolen the treasure and disappeared. One of these was **Neal Walker**.

Soon after this, a further storm wrecked another Spanish ship full of wine, brandy and dry goods 'upon one of the little Islands to the Leeward of this call'd the Camanas'. The crew of this boat reported that Neal Walker had taken the cargo for himself. Hunter wrote 'it seems he takes refuge in one of the aforementioned Islands. I shall do what I can to have him secured.' However, the Cayman Islands were searched from top to bottom by Governor Hunter's men, but nothing was found. What happened to the main part of the treasure from the *Genoesa* and the rest of the wine and brandy still remains a mystery, and joins the list of Caymanian pirate tales.

From 1730, the Jamaican courts became stiffer in their searching out and execution of pirates and their visitations became fewer on the Cayman Islands. At this time, permanent settlement began properly on Cayman and this was by individuals who wanted to create a quiet and steady life and, once settlement was well established on the islands, they became less open to pirate attack. There is no evidence that pirates actually settled on the Islands, as by their nature these men were wandering types and they had simply used the Islands as a base and a safe place to hide their treasure.

FIRST SETTLERS

Permanent settlement began between 1670 and 1730 and started in East End. The first recorded settler in this area was **Isaac Bodden**. He was born here around 1700 and married another Caymanian, Sarah Lamar in 1735. He is presumed to have been a grandson of Bodden, one of Oliver Cromwell's soldiers at the taking of Jamaica in 1655. Nathanial Glover, an American settled in Cayman, wrote in 1831:

> 'it is a well established fact that the first settlers were two soldiers from the disbanded army of Cromwell who came here about the year 1658 from Jamaica, whose names were Walter and Bowden, which plainly accounts for the numerous families of Watlers and Boddens throughout the Islands, the difference of the names only arising from some ignorant persons crossing the line Walter instead of the t and spelling Bodden with two D's instead of one. Be that as it may, Walter and Bowden came here for the purpose of catching turtle.'

This is how **Bodden Town**, then known as 'Old Isaacs' got it's name.

▲ Beach at Bodden Town

Early settlers consisted of shipwrecked sailors and buccaneers, Jamaican servants and runaway soldiers. These people became turtlers, farmers, mariners and logcutters. Day-to-day Caymanian life was quiet, very different from the swashbuckling tales of piracy. The men had a reputation as hardy and expert sailors.

Five large grants of land were given and recorded by the Jamaican authorities in 1735 and between 1741 and 1742. The grant in 1735 was for 3000 acres and was made to three people: Daniel Campbell, John Middleton and Mary Campbell. This was land on the North Sound which now stretches from Red Bay Estates, North Sound Way, the industrial park and airport, to Crewe Road and Hog Sty Bay in George Town. The grants of 1741–2 helped to ensure that the Islands remained a British colony during the war with Spain and France (1739–48). People found to be already established in these granted lands could keep them as long as they registered their claim within

▲ Natural Cayman

two years. This showed that, by this time, there was already a large amount of informal settlement. These grants went to Samuel Spofforth, Murray Crymble and William Foster. Samuel Spofforth, a prominent Bermudian ship owner with merchant connections in Jamaica who was also involved with the Cayman mahogany trade, was granted 1000 acres at West Bay. Crymble's land was between George Town and West Bay, behind Seven Mile Beach. William Foster's land stretched from George Town to Pull-and-Be-Damned Point near South Sound.

MAHOGANY TRADE

Records exist of a court case, in 1739, between William Foster and Benjamin Battersby over a mahogany trade matter. Battersby, during this case, gave an account of acquiring land:

'... when ever a person was intending to settle there with a Gang of Negroes to cutt mahogany the person so intending to Settle Chooses out a run of Land in which he puts his Slaves – and from thence the said Land belongs to and is deemed to be the property of the owner of the Slaves putt and Employed thereupon and the same is look't upon and Esteemed as the Sole and absolute property of the owner of such slaves and it is the Constant Agreement amongst all those who live on the said place not to Encroach of run in upon Each others run nor to remove or put out any persons Slaves who have so settled and the person so offending is look't and deemed upon as a great Trepasser and is made Liable to make satisfaction to the other person and the aforesaid usage and Custom is well known and Observed by all who live at the grand Caymanas'.

In the 1740s, the mahogany trade started in earnest between Jamaica and Cayman. In Michael Craton's book *Founded upon the Seas*, he says:

'In shipping registers the first vessel recorded as trading between Jamaica and the Cayman Islands was a 25 ton Bermuda sloop named the *Experiment* owned by Bermudian merchant Samuel Spofforth. It left Kingston for the 'Camanoes' on 21 Sep 1744 returned twelve weeks later with eighty one pieces of mahogany – cut from Spofforths land in West Bay'.

The sloop *Sarah* is recorded as making a similar trip in 1745. In 1763–4 there was much trade between Cayman and Jamaica when there was a convoy of mahogany carriers including the *Success* and the *Eagle*, each carrying 80 tons of timber. On 28 December 1765, Captain William Bodden, the first recorded Caymanian captain,

▲ The mahogany trade, as depicted in John Broad's 500-year mural in George Town

arrived on the schooner *Susanna* with a cargo of mahogany. Craton says that, on this voyage, Bodden was probably also carrying his son-in-law William Eden, the builder of Pedro Castle, with the intention of settling in Grand Cayman.

In 1765, Robert Christian of the ship *Active*, reckoned that there were about 100 free people and between 50 and 100 slaves. He also noted that there were about three or four Caymanian schooners employed in turtling and carrying mahogany to Jamaica.

The English surveyor **George Gauld** completed a map of Grand Cayman in 1773 showing some of the water depths at anchorages and in sounds. He explained that:

> '...when a vessel has the misfortune to be wrecked on this island some of the survivors generally chose to remain in a place where the necessaries of life are so easily acquired: beside several people from Jamaica and other places, who are involved in debt resort to the asylum where it is no easy matter to find them out, and bring them to justice. These accidental visitors frequently enter into matrimonial engagements and so become Settlers. ...
> though they are, in general poor, or rather content with what nature requires, yet Captain Bodden himself, and a few others are people of considerable property. They have about half a dozen Sloops and Schooners belonging to the Island, which they employ in turtling and trafficking to Jamaica'.

Gauld mentions that cotton and sugar were adequate for local consumption but resources of land, labour and capital were insufficient to establish sugar plantations like those in Jamaica. The inhabitants of Cayman lived in a state of nature. They produced corn, yams, sweet potatoes, cassava, breadfruit, pumpkins, plantains, bananas, pineapple, melons, limes and oranges. There were goats, cattle and horses but no sheep. There were only five families in Isaac Bodden's time but, by 1773, there were about 400 people.

▲ Soursop

▲ Pineapple

Accurate charts for navigating around the Cayman Islands were still being drawn up by the Royal Navy in the 1880s. British naturalists arrived to observe plants, birds, reptiles and molluscs. About 300 English settlers, expelled by the Spanish from Miskito Coast, came to Cayman in 1786 and 1787.

The Wreck of The Ten Sail

The Ten Sail was led by a recently captured French frigate *l'Inconstante*, renamed *HMS Convert* under the command of **Captain John Lawford** and comprised nine of the 58 merchant ships that the *Convert* was convoying from Jamaica back to Great Britain. *HMS Convert* left Port Royal for Bluefields Bay, also in Jamaica, on 28 January 1794. A week later, Captain Lawford led 32 ships to Long Bay (Negril) where they joined 26 more ships. Thus it was a huge fleet that set sail on Thursday, 6 February, expecting to pass well to the south of Grand Cayman. At midnight, six or seven of the ships moved ahead of the leading ship. They went unnoticed by the watch on the *Convert*. At 03.00 a distress gun went off and Captain Lawford heard 'Breakers ahead. Close to us' yelled by a watchman above. This was the breakers on the reef one mile away from Gun Bay, so named because of the large number of cannons salvaged from wreckage on the East End of Grand Cayman. Lawford explains:

'...as the Breakers appeared in every direction and I could not tell from the Darkness of the Night to what extent they might run, (I) deemed it most expedient to make the Signal for the Convoy to disperse and do the best for their own Safety that their own judgement could suggest, and as the Topsails were now sheeted home, the *Convert* would have certainly cleared the Breakers, if a Ship ahead had not unfortunately fallen on Board us, and before it was possible to extricate ourselves we got so near the Reefs, that all hopes of Clearing them vanished and she in a few moments struck, and very soon after Bilged.'

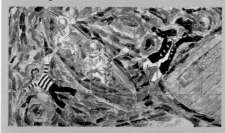

◀ Wreck of the *Ten Sail*
(John Broad's mural)

Old Isaacs was the closest community to the wreck sites and was populated by only three families. There had been a hurricane on 19 October that year, so provisions were scarce anyway. There were 400 survivors from the wrecked ships – the *Convert* alone had 280 people on board. The other ships in the convoy were *William and Elizabeth*, *Moorhall*, *Ludlow*, *Britannia*, *Richard*, *Nancy*, *Eagle*, *Sally* and *Fortune*. Captain Lawford recorded:

'the dawning of the day presented a most Melancholy scene, seven Ships and two Brigs on the same reef with the *Convert*, a very heavy sea running and the Wind blowing directly on the Shore; from the bad appearance of the Weather the Merchant Ships would not venture near enough to us to give any effectual assistance, and the ships on shore could not assist each other; I immediately ordered out the Boats to provide as far as possible for the safety of the Ships Company, the Masts were Cut away, and by unremitting exertions untill Night the whole of the Ships Company (excepting about Twenty who, as the Weather seemed to moderate, preferr'd staying on Board to the risqué of getting on Shore) were put on Board two or three Vessels that appeared at a great distance in the offing, or were put on the reef by means of rafts, &c. and taken up by Canoes'.

Only eight people drowned. Captain Lawford set out on foot for George Town three days after the wreck with two companions and a guide. This was a 31-hour journey on hot burning sands and sharp pointed coral rocks – very different from the road that takes only 25 minutes today! Distress messages were sent off to Jamaica, Havana and the Admiralty in London. Provisions arrived three weeks later and Lawford, who chose to remain in East End with several officers and 30 men in order to save as many stores as possible, camped in tents at Gun Bay for six weeks. *HMS Success* was sent to Grand Cayman to rescue Captain Lawford and his men. The *Success* arrived in mid-March 1794 and took Lawford to Port Royal. He was then court-martialled and acquitted. The court martial summed up the misfortune by stating the strong current, which made the ships veer further northward than they had thought. Lawford went on to enjoy a distinguished career, became an admiral and was finally knighted.

A warning to mariners was published a year later explaining that off the east end of Grand Cayman is a reef which runs about three quarters of a mile into the sea and which is very low and dangerous, especially at night, because, as it is unseen, it makes you think you are clear of the island, but you are not – by that time it is too late to steer off to safety.

Lawford's men had salvaged what they could and then authorised Governor Bodden and partner Robert Clarke to be appointed as official salvors. In the area known as Gun Bay, *Ten Sail* is the wreck around which legends have grown up. There was supposed to be a prince aboard the fleet and King George III of England granted Caymanians freedom from taxation in recognition of their bravery during the rescue and salvage – though this was probably more to keep the islands loyal to the British throne. The wreck sites were searched by local islanders for valuables which included lengths of cloth used for clothing, sails, rope, blocks, tackle, carpenters' tools, ammunition, swords, pistols, pikes, axes and cannons.

In the late 1970s, coral-encrusted cannon began to appear outside hotels and houses on Grand Cayman. Some were dated 1781 and marked with the fleur-de-lis, suggesting that

these had come from the original French ship, the *Convert*. In 1980, divers were still finding wreckage that could have been part of the *Ten Sail*. Naval hardware and pottery shards were found in the area that had been Lawford's salvage camp near the freshwater vent Mermaid Springs.

Monument Park, to commemorate the wreck of the Ten Sail, was opened by HM Queen Elizabeth II in February 1994, 200 years after the disaster. The commemorative plaque stands on Gun Bluff overlooking the reefs into which the ships crashed.

▲ Plaque to commemorate the wreck of the *Ten Sail*

GOVERNMENT

In 1800, Governor Bodden set up the first militia and the first churches and schools were run by Anglican and Methodist Ministers. There were no large plantations on Cayman as the fertile land is only to be found in small pockets, so the social division was less distinct here than on other Caribbean islands. Men were away at sea, so women played the strongest part within the community. According to the census of 1802, 933 slaves cleared trails and felled and sawed trees for the mahogany trade. Houses were normally single-storey and were built with a local hardwood frame with wattle and plaster walls. Roofs were thatched and windows were just holes in the wall with no glass, but had shutters or louvres. The verandahs that one sees now on traditional Caymanian houses probably became commonplace in the 1900s. William Eden's Great Pedro, built in 1780, was a three-storey, stone building.

According to Craton's book, goods exported from Grand Cayman are illustrated by the cargo of William Bodden's *Susan & Kitty* in November 1811 on its way to Kingston: 19 bags of cotton, 12 barrels, 10 baskets, six baskets of corn, two barrels of tortoiseshell, one mahogany log, six hundredweight of corned fish, an anchor, 12 hundredweight of old copper and 18 puncheons of rum (wreck goods). An example of imported goods that were on William Bodden's *Charming Kitty* that arrived from Kingston in November 1809 included: two barrels of sugar, six trunks, six boxes, one basket, and a small quantity of loose dry goods, one basket, five tubs of 'crockeryware', one barrel of flour,

▲ Pedro Castle

three firkins of butter, three barrels each of beef and pork, one box each of raisins and currants, one small box of tobacco, one small box of bottled liquor, a cask of rum and six barrels of bread.

Government became more formal with the legislature meeting at William Eden's Great Pedro on 5 December 1831. The Legislature then consisted of a magistrate and five appointed councillors. Its organisation was similar to that in Jamaica – a council with representatives from each district to form local laws for better government. Here, there were two representatives from each of the five districts: West Bay, George Town, South Sound, Prospect and Bodden Town. These ten representatives met for the first time in George Town on 31 December 1831. Eight magistrates met at the same time, in a different room, and no law was considered valid until it had the assent of both houses. This was the same as the British system.

In April 1834, an edict freed all slaves, and a census was carried out by James Minot Jr in order to calculate the compensation payouts. This recorded 984 slaves, most of them living in Bodden Town. In 1841, Nathaniel Glover, who was an American who had lived in Bodden Town since 1831, gave an interesting picture of Cayman:

'Slavery only existed here by name. The owners generally were over ndulgent and the children of slaves were usually brought up in the houses of their master and were often playmates to their children. They were much better provided for then that they are now since they became free. When I first came to the island in 1831 it was a second Eden and I thought it was impossible to have found a happier set of people. It was a delightful ride from Bodden Town to George Town. The negroes' provision grounds lined each side of the road and the trees were bending with their ripe and yellow fruits. An instance of thieving from each other was scarcely ever heard of'.

Emancipation was at midnight on 31 July 1834 and was supposed to be followed by a period of apprenticeship during which the apprentices would be paid by their former owners to work for a further six years. This system was designed to ease the transition from slavery to full freedom.

Lord Sligo, the Jamaican Governor, visited Grand Cayman in September 1834. He had sent 30 men from the West India regiment to keep the peace and he swore in local justices of the peace who were to award slave compensation to their owners. He wrote an account of Cayman and its people. He found the island rich and fertile and 'covered with the most luxuriant Herbage'. There were self-sufficient farmers producing tobacco, cotton and maize and there were horses, mules and cattle. Mosquitoes he describes as 'quite a national misfortune'. He recorded the population as 'almost one thousand white persons and almost nine hundred apprentices' which, as he wrote to his colonial secretary, were 'In point of stature and make, I hardly ever saw a finer race of men, their average height certainly very much exceeds that of any other country I have seen'.

◀ Horse

In Bodden Town, where there was the densest concentration of former slaves, the chief focus of social tension emerged. The people there were either sullen and listless or very wild in their demonstration of joy, shouting, fiddling, dancing and drinking to excess. West Bay was more peaceful than Bodden Town.

Grand Cayman's main residents hated the presence of the West India Regiment and behaved badly towards the soldiers and towards their own former slaves. This was part of the reason for the quick end to apprenticeships which was initially enforced by British soldiers in April 1835. Thus, the apprenticeship system ceased after only 10 months, not six years as elsewhere, and many former slaves found land for themselves in North Side and East End. They became self-sufficient farmers and built totally independent lives. This was swift change for a normally slow and steadily moving island.

After emancipation, some former slaves migrated to the Bay Islands of Honduras. Britain declared these islands a colony between 1852 and 1859. Others migrated to Belize and the Miskito Coast of Nicaragua, San Andres, Old Providence, Corn Island and the Isle of Pines.

However, sometimes ex slaves and ex masters worked together on catching turtles. The profits were divided up – most going to the boat owner and captain. Custos John Drayton explained that:

'… the crew gets the one half of the profits and the owner the other. All the hands have share and share alike whether Black or White, excepting the Commander who has a different allowance out of the owners share. Formerly they (the slaves) had what their master chose to give them; some one quarter some one third of what White hired hands had. But since they have become free they share alike and there is not difficulty in obtaining hands'.

Everyone had to rely on a subsistence economy, the turtling industry, shipbuilding and wrecking. Among West Indian cultures, Caymanians were among the boldest seafarers. Many Caribbean fishermen stayed close to home as their islands had more fertile land from which food could be produced. Caymanians ventured much further afield to bring home money for their families as they had to depend more upon the sea as a route to survival.

The compensation for slaves, which must have been in excess of £20000 brought about an economy based more on cash than on barter. Ex slave owners were now free to start up shipbuilding, turtling and shopkeeping businesses. They now had cash to pay for workers.

Many former slave owners migrated to Belize, the Miskito Coast of Nicaragua, San Andres, Corn Island, the Isle of Pines, Tampa, Mobile and Port Arthur. The second migration was after 1831 to the Bay Islands, Utila, Roatan and Guanaja close to the northern shore of Honduras. In 1859, these islands became part of Honduras so all the Caymanians there came back home.

WRECKING

Most wrecked ships came from Jamaica. The Cayman Islands were not properly charted and the ironshore reefs surrounding the islands were deadly. One man's misfortune became the Caymanians' providence and wrecking, the process of salvaging valuables from a wrecked ship, became a livelihood – the wreckers' terms were half of all the valuables of the ship and cargo. The Caymanians were also prepared to risk their own lives saving people on board and proved very kind.

A Presbyterian missionary, Hope Masterton Waddell, was on a ship that was wrecked on the East End reef and spent 10 days on the island in January 1845. This is what he recorded:

'… When day dawned, a small low island was visible at some distance, and between it and the reef a lagoon of smooth water.

Ere long, to our great joy, canoes were seen coming off from the shore. 'What a benevolent people,' I said; 'see how they hasten to our help.' 'Wreckers,' said our captain 'that must be their trade. Many vessels have been brought up here all standing;' and he pointed to anchors, chain cables, and fragments of ships lying on the reef, over which the water now lay calm and clear. A fleet of canoes was making for us, and soon surrounded our helpless craft; when a host of wild, reckless-looking coloured men sprang up the sides, like pirates or boarders greedy for prey. The head man, advancing to the captain, with one word of pity and two of business, agreed to take everything ashore, on the usual terms of a half for their trouble.

Then began the work of despoiling the vessel. The fellows were up the rigging, and over the spars, and everywhere in a moment. Down came the sails and ropes, bundled into the canoes, and off ashore with amazing rapidity. Up came everything from the hold. The cabin doors, fittings, and furnishings, were by fair or foul means torn off and sent away. The people seemed to vie which would do most, the canoes which would go and return most quickly, striving to strip the wreck during the calm of the morning, before the sea breeze rising should impede their operations. Some of them were swearing shockingly until rebuked; when they looked surprised, begged pardon, and then shouted to their companions to mind themselves, as there was a 'parson on board'.

The head wrecker let Waddell and his family stay in his house, which was the only two-storey building at East End. Waddell went to George Town to attend the public sale of the wreck goods. He said that George Town 'presented an attractive appearance in a line of good houses fronting the bay'. And that one of the Caymanian women explained that because there was a lack of fertile land they went 'fishing especially for turtle, to supply the English ships, but to tell you the truth, sir, our main dependence is on wrecks. And we all thank God when a ship comes ashore'.

Even though, in 1820, Captain Lloyd of *HMS Parthian* had written in his logbook that the position was incorrect, the chart supplied by the British Royal Navy until the 1850s plotted the Cayman Islands much further to the west than they actually were. This did not help a captain's navigation around the treacherous reefs. As divers will tell you, there is a sharp drop down the wall before the reefs start so, if the captain had measured the depth and thought he was alright, the very next minute his boat would have run aground on the especially sharp ironshore which surrounds all three islands. The Cayman Islands have always been a trap for ships. Today, divers can explore the many wreck sites surrounding the three islands.

In the case of ships in trouble around the Islands, one person's misfortune became another's fortune, and legend has it on all three islands (as in many coasts around the world) that, at night, rather than warning approaching ships of the reefs, watchmen are said to have walked the coast with a torch or lantern to make ships' captains think that the slowly moving light was another ship under way and thus cause them to sail into the reef.

Wrecks

There are many wreck tales and one was about the *Curacao*, a merchant vessel that crashed violently onto Cayman Brac Bluff in 1915. Wreckage and bodies were flung far and wide. Five gallon tins of kerosene were found along the top of the bluff. Tins of kerosene were also found floating ashore at East End on Grand Cayman. For months following the foundering of the *Curacao* lamps in the houses of both islands burned brightly.

There is a legend which explains the name 'Rum Point'. In the eighteenth century, a ship was wrecked on Cayman reefs before Christmas. The cargo was rum from sugar plantations on nearby islands. Today villagers of East End repeat the tale of a procession of barrels of rum from Rum Point to East End. Barrels were being given out to families and friends along the way. The owners of carts were said to be totally incoherent by the end of the journey and the rest of the island's population in various stages of intoxication. That year saw an excellent Christmas celebration!

The *Dend* was another memorable wreck in 1846 at East End. This ship was loaded with valuable dry goods which the islanders badly needed as they had suffered a major hurricane that year. Everyone was bolstered by news of the wreck because there was at last plenty to eat and wear.

In April 1874 the British barque *Iphigenia* crashed at a reef near Bodden Town. The wreckers were so aggressive in their demands for 50 per cent of all the salvaged goods, even when the ship had not been very badly damaged, that it led to the 1875 Wrecking and Salvage Law – giving more rights to unfortunate captains wrecked on the Islands' reefs. Individuals with the title 'Receivers of Wreck' were appointed in the Cayman Islands, Turks and Caicos Islands and Jamaica. However, in September 1888, another ship, the Norwegian *Juga*, struck the Bodden Town reef and the boat was met with the same very efficient, although not particularly welcome, wrecking by the Caymanians. Captain Jacobsen, like other captains before him, was trying to preserve as much of the wreckage before the wreckers could take it all away. Captain Rolfe of *HMS Pylades*, who investigated the case, commented 'Wrecking is one of the principal industries of the Cayman Islands, and one which they appear thoroughly to understand and to conduct in a straightforward and equitable manner'. By 1910 wrecking was no longer such an important industry, mostly because maps had improved and there was less chance of shipwrecks.

Evidence of the heritage of wrecking is to be found if you look carefully all over the three islands. Some houses are built from pieces saved from shipwrecks, some floors of houses are covered with French tiles, and one house has a mahogany staircase saved from a German ship. A hut on Little Cayman is built from keel timbers. The *Oro Verde,* which was wrecked on the island, was stripped and towed into deep water as a diving attraction. The main derrick and boom was sent to the Brac to be used as a crane in the government dock.

Anchors and cannons were very valuable items gained from wrecking. The Caymanian Heritage Trust at the National Museum has a fine collection of objects obtained from the many ships that have foundered around the Islands over the years.

Modern life in Cayman has brought air transportation, offshore finance, banking and, of course, tourism and has shifted Caymanian focus from the sea to other occupations. But the tradition of wrecking is still seen after storms when locals closely explore and search the beaches for any objects that may have been washed up.

▲ Cannons at Mermaid Lane in East End

PROGRESS

Before 1900 change was very slow. The Jamaican and British Governments spent no money on the Cayman Islands to assist change or advancement and ignored them as much as possible. The Cayman Islands became a dependency of Jamaica in an Act passed in the Westminster Parliament in June 1863. The 54-member Caymanian Assembly was democratic, representing all districts, classes and races but the merchants and shipowners held most of the power. In 1920, the first steam ships started arriving at Grand Cayman.

Jamaica also ignored the Cayman Islands as much as possible to avoid any expense and the only advantage of being a dependency of Jamaica was that tonnage dues were not payable. But Jamaica did pass laws for good government, peace and order and the local legislature was recognised. This organised the police's use of public property, the construction of public utilities including roads and the cleansing of streets. The Caymanian Assembly controlled its own revenue expenditure. Local laws had to be signed by Jamaica and were subject to disallowance by Britain.

Nowadays, Cayman is still inextricably linked to the ocean for income and Caymanians rely on the sea as a conduit for produce and the luxurious standard of living most are now used to. Tourists come to swim and snorkel in the dazzling blue, crystalline waters and divers to have world class experiences. Stingray City is world famous – there the sea is at its most turquoise.

TURTLING

Originally, the remote and undisturbed coasts of the Cayman Islands were ideal nesting beaches for these free swimming reptiles, with the low and sandy shores and the rich submarine pastures providing plenty of nourishing herbage. But, by the end of the 1600s, due to Jamaican schooners having 'fished out' the local waters, Caymanians had to travel to Cuba and then the Nicaragua Quays. Each turtle could supply a great quantity of fresh meat. The turtles could be kept alive on board ship, so sailors could have fresh meat as a change from salted, pickled beef or pork which became rotten before the voyage was over.

Green turtles, so called because of the greenish colour of the body and the largest of which might be 1.5 metres (4 feet) long and weigh 500 lbs were the most valuable. A **hawksbill turtle** was a good catch but the fishermen did not want **leatherbacks** or **loggerheads** as their flesh and shells were not worth anything. The green turtle has great powers of navigation. It can survive up to five hours with

no oxygen in its system, and its heartbeats can be nine minutes apart. Their long range, homing sense allows them to return to the same beach on which they were born for breeding.

◀ Turtles

Turtling

Caymanian turtlers separated into three or more catboat crews and found the turtles using a water glass. This was a square wooden box with an open top and a clear pane of glass inserted into a groove at the bottom. It could be partly immersed in the sea to find turtles which were often sleeping at night in the narrow reefs, sand and coral channels. Two sorts of net were used to spread over the carefully selected area: a swing net which was 10 to 13 fathoms in length and anchored at one end to allow it to swing with the current; and long nets which were anchored at both ends and much larger, measuring 4 by 12 or 8 by 30 fathoms and attached to a hand rope buoyed with floats so that they would run parallel to the surface of the water. A piece of wood carved into the shape of a turtle was attached to the net. Thatch rope was originally used for the 10-inch mesh, but the nets were later made out of cotton line.

▲ Catboat crews as depicted in Randy Cholette's painting 'Jeanie of the Judge'

The turtlers would set between 10 and 30 nets and, as the sleeping turtles rose to the surface, they would struggle as they came into contact with the nets and thus entangle themselves. At dawn, the nets would be pulled into the boats as quickly as possible so that the nets were not torn on the coral. A good catch would be of about 8–10 turtles. Sometimes, a conical-shaped trap net with six-inch mesh was used. This was lowered quietly into the water, weighted at the base by an iron ring 1.5–2 metres (5–7 feet) in diameter. The net was open at the bottom and attached to a line at the top. The net was totally controlled by the trapper and could be dropped over a turtle at the right moment.

When the turtles were on board, each was spancelled, which constituted piercing its flippers with a hot poker and tying the front and back limbs together with a thatch rope. The initials of the schooner's name were then cut into the bottom shell of each turtle to mark out the catch. The turtles had to be placed upside down so that their lungs wouldn't collapse from the pressure of the top shell and body weight against the soft, bottom shell. Wedges were put under the shell to prevent rolling and a wooden pillow placed underneath the turtle's head. The catch was taken to a crawl where two men would look after all the catch until there were enough (100–350 turtles) to return home. A crawl was made by sticking mangrove saplings into a soft area of seabed in about five feet of water and tying them together with thatch rope. The pens were about 60 metres (20 feet) square with a gate at one side where the turtles could be taken in or out.

At the end of the season, which would last about three months, the turtles had to be lassooed out and put on board ship to be sold directly to American traders in the Miskito Cays, passing ships, the markets in Kingston, Jamaica, Key West, Tampa or at home in the Cayman Islands where there was a crawl at North Sound. The profits from their sale were split into two parts – one half being given to the owner of the schooner, the other half being divided between the captain and his crew. While they were away, the turtlers' family would have been buying everything they could not grow or make themselves (e.g. flour, sugar and cloth) from the stores on a credit system booked to the name of the man who was away at sea. They were expected to settle the accounts on return. They could only hope that they had earned enough to cover the debt.

FARMING

Turtlers spent part of the year at sea and the rest ashore as farmers. While back at home in Cayman, the men joined the whole family in their efforts to produce enough food for themselves and a small surplus to use as barter for items they could not grow or make themselves, such as sugar, coffee beans, flour, rice, canned meat, cutlery, crockery, glassware, lanterns, liquid fuel, medicines, and ready-made clothes. Some had canoes to transport provisions around the island, but most simply walked, carrying loads in baskets with a broad strap across their foreheads, not on their heads like Jamaicans. Only the very prosperous settlers rode horses. It was considered a great luxury to be able to raise cattle for beef and milk, but most kept

▲ Cassava and other produce   ▲ Goat

pigs, chickens and goats and occasionally caught wild birds, crabs, lobsters and agouti.

Most people ate fish and conch and starchy food such as cassava, potatoes, corn, beans, and squash, yams, cocoas, breadfruit, bananas, plantains, coconuts and sugarcane. There were also pineapples, mangoes and some citrus fruits, so the diet was very healthy. The men fished, cut wood, cleared the bush, dug, carried loads, built homes and maintained the tools. The women looked after the children, ran the household, prepared the food, made, washed and mended the clothes. They also often had a kitchen garden and went to market to sell whatever the family had produced. Children also had their tasks; they swept the yards with thatch brooms, carried water and helped to make cassava flour and to grind corn. They also stripped thatch leaves and twisted the strands, did the weeding, looked after the animals and collected firewood. Mosquitoes were plentiful, so fires had to be lit because the smoke kept them away. There was plenty to be done within the family to keep everything running smoothly.

Although life was hard work, the islands were as beautiful as they are today with the sunshine, white sand and turquoise waters.

SHIPBUILDING

Brave, resilient and very independent, the Caymanians depended on their ships for income, import and export, communication and transportation. The Cayman Islanders were very outward looking, as they had to be adventurers to bring home enough to keep their families. Early craft were simple dugout canoes sometimes with a mast and sail. Later, they developed the building of a specialised craft that was immensely easy to manoevre and suitable for both local fishing and for loading onto schooners for the voyages hundreds of miles from home. This was the Cayman catboat, swift and durable, and was first built in 1904 by Daniel Jervis, a turtling captain from

Cayman Brac. Native hardwoods were used for building the boat and silver thatch palms for the rope. They had to have small boats to be able to enter shallow lagoons and the cat boats were both light and easy to navigate.

▲ John Broad's mural of shipbuilding

Mahogany, cedar and other hardwood saplings were ideal for making the curved timbers. Floor frames were sawn or steamed to fit the internal shape of the hull and were fastened to the keel stem and sternpost with tree nails and copper nails from Jamaica and, later, brass screws. The catboat was 5 metres (16 feet) long and 1.5 metres (4 feet) wide and drew 45 centimetres (18 inches) of water. There was no deep keel or centreboard. It was double ended with a mast in the centre and a rudder for sailing. Painted a distinctive bright blue colour, named 'catboat blue', this provided camouflage when viewed from below by turtles. The oars were normally made from Spanish elm and white pine and there was a calabash bailer to scoop out water if necessary. These boats were carried on a larger vessel such as a schooner to the turtling grounds and unloaded upon arrival at the chosen destination – often as far as the Miskito Cays which was a 700 mile round trip – so the crews could go their separate ways for their catches.

◄ Randy Chollette's painting of catboats

Shipbuilding was one of the Caymans' proudest achievements. Compensation for slavery, estimated at £20000 between slave owners, had allowed shipbuilding ventures. Most turtling schooners were of between 40 and 50 tons, designed and built from a half model (three quarters of an inch to a foot) which was carved from cedar with sharp pieces of glass. This was cut into sections so the increasing and decreasing shapes of the frames of the hull could be measured and made. The schooners were usually 21 metres (70 feet) in length. The sailcloth, fasteners and tackle were imported from the US and the anchors and the cable came from Jamaica. The vessels took eight or 10 men from six months to a year to build. At first, they were built purely for turtling and then later for freighting, and sometimes the boats were sold to Cuba or the US as fishing ships.

Family names traditionally associated with shipbuilding were Arch, Bodden and Ebanks and, on the Brac, Bodden, Foster, Scott and Tibbetts. When it was time for a schooner to be launched, the whole island would get together to help and to celebrate the occasion – it was a party atmosphere. The launching of boats such as the schooner *Goldfield* were island-wide events. The boats were eased down on their sides, gradually cutting away the shoring under the hull. Thatch palm logs were placed as rollers underneath. It was the tradition, and a sign of good luck, to have a lady break a bottle against the boat before it sailed.

In the 1930s Grand Cayman owned 23 schooners and 300 catboats. In 1935 the regatta in Cayman was introduced by the commissioner, Sir Allen Cardinall, with cash prizes for the winning boats. This was timed for the last week in January, between the turtling seasons, and was intended to increase the marketing of Cayman-built boats.

The *Goldfield*, which won the regatta three years in a row (1936–38) was known as the last great Caymanian schooner. It was 25.8 metres (86 feet) long, 6.6 metres (22 feet) wide with a 21 metre (7 foot) draft and was built in 1929 using Caymanian mahogany and yellow pine by **James N Arch** for **William Conwell Watler** (1869–1931). The shipyard was on the site of the present day Hard Rock Café in George Town. Launched in July 1930, the 100-ton vessel was used for turtling on the Miskito coast. Early one morning, during a storm in September 1937, the *Goldfield* arrived in George Town from Tampa with its cargo and passengers. The passengers were landed despite the wind and high seas but the much-needed provisions had to be left on board. During the night, the continuing storm broke the mooring lines and the *Goldfield* was swept out to sea. The British warship *HMS Orion* went out to search for the ship and found it drifting, but undamaged, in the open sea. The crew re-boarded and all the goods were saved.

The *Goldfield* carried goods to the US during World War II. She was a much loved schooner and was relied upon by Caymanians for importing goods, their post and bringing their families home. In 1958 the *Goldfield* was sold to a merchant in Colombia who used her to export coconuts, and was subsequently found in Seattle in 1983. It was de-masted in the Pacific and the hull returned to Grand Cayman in 1986, but she sank before funds could be raised to restore her and her remains are in North Sound to this day.

The *Cimboco* was the first local boat to have an engine. It weighed 120 tons and was built in 1927 by the **Cay**man **I**slands **M**otor **Bo**at **Co**mpany – the bold letters show how the boat was named. Its first trip carried 20 first class passengers, 12 deck passengers and, with a crew of 11, ran a service between Grand Cayman, Little Cayman, Cayman Brac and Kingston Jamaica three times a week. This continued for 20 years. The *Lady Slater* was the second motorised ship built in Grand Cayman. The launches of both boats caused island-wide celebration. The two boats were constructed by Captain **Rayal Bodden** in his shipyard in North Church Street, George Town. They were used to take goods, passengers and mail between Grand Cayman, Cayman Brac Jamaica and the Tampa. Rayal B Bodden also built the Peace Memorial, the Town Hall, the Elmslie Memorial Church, the Library and the Post Office using hardwoods and hand moulded concrete blocks.

THATCH ROPE

One of the important Caymanian industries was the making of very strong rope from the leaves of the silver thatch palm *Coccothrinax proctori*. The palm is native only to the Cayman Islands and the leaves were used for roofing houses, making brooms, fans, hats and the baskets that everyone used for carrying root vegetables. The rope was twisted in a wooden winch from three strands of the unopened leaf shoots into lengths of 25 fathoms. Known on the islands as 'tatch', it was coiled up and taken to market. This was a labour-intensive process which involved the cutting, drying, stripping, laying out and twisting of the silver thatch leaves, but it was worth it as, at the time, 100 yards fetched nine pence and you could buy cloth for nine pence a yard, a bottle of kerosene for six pence and sugar for a penny per pound. The rope was exported to Jamaica. It was excellent for use on boats and for making turtle nets since it was very resistant to damage by salt water.

◀ Man wearing a thatch hat and making thatch sandals

STAMPS

The postal service in Cayman was very popular as there were large numbers of Caymanians living abroad and letters were the only means of communication for most people. It was a great source of revenue to the Islands. The state income from stamps rose from £769 in 1909–10 to £2750 in 1913–14 and equalled the revenue from direct taxation.

The first Post Office in George Town was opened in 1889 but Jamaican stamps had to be used until the first Cayman Islands' stamp with the head of Queen Victoria was issued in 1900.

Sometimes, stamps were overprinted or misprinted and became very valuable and collectable. In 1907, when the halfpenny stock of Edward VII stamps had run out, Jamaica allowed Cayman to print them over sheets of the penny issue. The most sought after overprint was issued in November 1907 when Miss Gwendolyn Parsons, the postmistress in Grand Cayman overprinted the 1½d values on sheets of the five-shilling stamps. In February 1908, the local Police Inspector, J H O'Sullivan, altered four sheets of 4d stamps by hand to read 2½d. Most of these stamps were bought up at the time as an investment and were not actually used for posting letters.

Pictorial stamps were first used in 1935. They portrayed the red footed booby, the hawksbill turtle and conch shells. The Cayman Islands' stamps always have very striking designs. Sometimes, commemorative stamps celebrating British royal occasions or events from British or Caymanian history are issued.

Progress made by commissioners
Edmund Parsons was the last Custos, and the first paid Chief Executive of Government from 1888–98. He kept accurate records of births, marriages and deaths and maintained good contact with Jamaica. The Post Office was established at this time. Parsons made sure that the Islands took part in the Jamaica Exhibition of 1891 as a publicity exercise. This was a showcase for the natural products and crafts of the island that foreigners had previously not known much about or even heard of. It was a chance to tell everyone about the warm but healthy climate, the beautiful villages surrounded by pure white sandy beaches, and to explain that most

▲ Joanne Sibley's painting 'Boggy Sand Road' showing early Cayman life in the villages people owned their homes no matter how big or small, so rent was unknown. The brochure also explained that

'Besides their profession as seamen, however, they are good tillers of the soil and the same individual is at one period of the year a seaman braving the perils of the ocean and at another remains at home and cultivates the soil in order to provide for the wants of his family.'

Frederick Shedden Sanguinetti (1898–1906) took up what was now a new post. He became a full-time Commissioner, Treasurer, Chief Justice and President of the Legislative Council. He carried on the efficiency and good record-keeping of Parsons. Sanguinetti introduced the first typewriter for correspondence. His tenure must have been hard and unrewarding as he had to deal with the disease that destroyed most of the coconut palms – the export of coconuts had been big business. Fortunately, it was able to continue on Cayman Brac. He also sought to establish salt, brick, cotton and phosphate industries, but his endeavours came to nothing. The Islands' revenue was not enough to support his efforts to encourage education and health care. There was no local taxation and revenue was only obtained from the 5 per cent duty levied on imports e.g. four shillings a gallon on distilled spirits, and the postage stamp revenue. There was also the turtling dispute over fishing license fees in the Miskito Cays, which had been controlled by Nicaragua since 1895. This problem was not resolved until Hirst's time in 1916.

Saguinetti, as Commissioner of Grand Cayman, visited the Sister Islands a few times. In 1902, he commented that 'Everything betokened an orderly, contented community'. He noted the successful coconut industry:

'Business seemed brisk. There has been a very large coconut crop, such as has not borne for years, and the carrying capacity of the Island vessels to deal with the export of nuts has been scarcely sufficient. . . . I estimate that one million nuts have been shipped between October and February last. . . . A sudden increase in price has further stimulated the trade, a large portion of which is done with Mobile.'

The Coconut industry on Cayman Brac flourished between 1890 and 1915, until a very bad hurricane on Friday, 13 August 1915 destroyed most of the trees and the coconut disease from Grand Cayman killed off the rest. Sanguinetti also noted the fine shipbuilding on Cayman Brac:

'There are at present three vessels on the Stocks at Cayman Brac, beautiful models of sailing craft. One of these vessels will be of 290 tons, the largest ever built in Caymanas. I am glad to notice that many of the smaller vessels built from time to time are sailed over to Cuba and sold at paying prices for the local coasting trade and fishery. The large quantity of native lumber encourages the enterprise.'

George Stevenson Shirt Hirst took up office as Commissioner in March 1907. Hirst had studied Medicine at Edinburgh University and was employed as both Commissioner and the government Medical Officer. He had been a Medical Officer in The Gold Coast and in the Turks and Caicos Islands. His salary was £500 per annum and a Government residence and offices were built for him. He designed these himself and developed George Town into a proper colonial capital. He also laid out the main roads that still exist today such as Mary Street and Elgin Avenue and the public park which was opposite Government House on Elgin Avenue. The park originally staged the Agricultural Show – now a firm tradition in Grand Cayman – which is now held at the Agricultural Pavilion in Savannah.

Hirst was responsible for widening the roads in Grand Cayman at the waterfront and Shedden Road, which he continued up to Bodden Town, was named after his predecessor Frederick Shedden Sanguinetti. A driveable road was built for seven miles to West Bay and North Sound. Crewe Road was named after Lord Elgin's successor as British Colonial Secretary and roads to Savannah and Newlands were also built at this time. On Boxing Day 1909, a bicycle race was held on the newly-built road between George Town and Bodden Town. Hirst produced the *Handbook of the Cayman Islands* in 1907 and 1908 and *Notes on the History of the Cayman Islands* in 1910 which was a result of his study of the islands while he was Commissioner. It included information about Cayman family history and reproductions of 19th century documents.

The National Revenue was £2000 annually under Sanguinetti and rose to £4000 with Hirst as Commissioner. Hirst developed the police force and an internal postal service. In 1907, the head of the police, previously called Sergeant Major, became the Inspector and four permanent constables and eight district constables were enrolled. All policemen were postmen and also carried out customs duties. Apart from a few tensions which arose largely because of Hirst's Catholicism, and which were sorted out by Governor Olivier of Jamaica, Hirst is remembered for his energies in modernising Cayman.

▲ Policeman in George Town

Hugh Houston Hutchings took over as Commissioner in 1919 until 1931. He was born in 1869 on the Turks and Caicos Islands. By this time the revenue was between £6000 and £8000 per year. He organised Rayal Bodden to build the Peace Memorial in George Town which was officially opened on 11 November 1926. By the mid-1930s there were seven lorries, five motor cycles and 41 cars but the main roads were still just sandy lanes. There was both a postal and a telephone service between West Bay, George Town and Bodden Town. The post was delivered in a vehicle which was also a nine-passenger bus. This was the time when Rayal Bodden's boats the *Cimboco* and *Lady Slater* and another boat the *Nunoca*, built by Heber Arch Sr, commenced their voyages between Kingston, Grand Cayman and Tampa.

▲ Rayal Bodden's Peace Memorial, George Town

During prohibition (1919–33) smuggling liquor helped the National Revenue, though Cayman did not indulge in the activity as much as the Bahamas whose revenue from the re-exports of liquor rose from almost nothing in 1918 to over £1 000 000 in 1923. Caymanians did not approve of this activity and Hutchings managed to find a way round the problem. A law was passed by the Assembly in 1923 which allowed wines and spirits free entry to the Cayman Islands and imposed a duty of 2s 6d a gallon when being re-exported. This filled the waterfront in George Town with barrels of liquor and faced much opposition from Presbyterian and Baptist ministers, but, for a time, swelled the National Revenue. This was a short-lived enterprise and by 1926, on advice from Governor Edward Stubbs of Jamaica, it came to an end.

Allen Wolsey Cardinall was Commissioner from 1934 to 1941. He was born in 1887 and was educated at Winchester College in England. He had been Assistant District Commissioner on the Gold Coast for 18 years and arrived in George Town on 14 February 1834. Cardinall Avenue, today one of the smartest shopping streets in George Town, is named after him. Cardinall was responsible for important modernisations in promoting tourism, radio and communications generally. He received a knighthood in 1943 for patriotism and hope during World War II.

He and his colleague, Aston Rutty on Cayman Brac, thought up the idea for a Cayman sailing regatta, which started in 1935. Being a sportsman, he saw that an annual regatta would show off the islands' superb boatbuilding and excellent sailing skills. The regatta would also attract yachtsmen from abroad who might well become valuable customers. The Cayman Islands Yacht and Sailing Club was also set up, starting with a membership of 73. By 1937, this had doubled.

The Chamber of Commerce was also founded in 1935 and Cardinall wrote promotional articles about the Islands to encourage tourists. On 22 February 1937 the *SS Atlantis* cruise liner arrived at George Town. About 340 passengers came to visit the island to swim in the incredibly clear, turquoise sea, drink cocktails, rum and beer, eat ice cream and buy tortoiseshell, sharkskin, thatch-work, postcards and silver and gold coins said to have been buried pirate treasure. Visiting a turtle crawl was one of the tourist attractions and there was also a catboat demonstration. The Cayman Islands Hotels Aid Law 1937 encouraged hotel building by waiving any duty on building materials.

At this time shark fishing became a supplement to turtling and, in 1935, about 12 000 shark skins were sold for a good price to the US. Cardinall researched and found ways of selling the flesh, oil and liver of the sharks.

▲ Elmslie Memorial Church

▲ Public Library

Cardinall instigated the first radio stations on Grand Cayman and Cayman Brac and the automatic lighthouses at East End, South West Point, George Town and North West Point on Grand Cayman and on the east point of Cayman Brac and the west point of Little Cayman. Roads were built from Bodden Town to East End and from Frank Sound across the island to North Side. There was also a road built on Cayman Brac. Rayal Bodden, who had built the Peace Memorial and the Elmslie Memorial Church under commissioner Hutchings, now built a hospital, the Public Library and the Post Office which were both finished by 1939.

WORLD WAR II

During World War II, Caymanians gained employment with the British Merchant Service as seamen and some were more directly involved in the war, either in the Jamaican Defence Force, the Royal Navy, Royal Air Force or the Trinidad Royal Naval Volunteer Reserve (TRNVR). Some were gunners on ships that went far afield and some crewed the U-boat patrols in the Eastern Caribbean.

1942 saw the arrival of the American base at George Town. It was used as a refuelling stop for ships that patrolled for submarines and seaplanes. The fact that the shipping lanes between the Cayman Islands, Jamaica and the US were protected by American Forces meant that there was no food shortage. Thatch rope was in high demand, so the women making it were kept very busy. Rayal Bodden built two 162-ton minesweepers for the Royal Navy. The government gained much revenue from the duty on the increased number of imported goods. World War II was a time of high employment and income for the Caymanians and set them on the road to further development.

Commissioner Jones took over from Cardinall in 1941. On 14 May 1942, the *Cimboco* had to rescue survivors from a steamer *Camayagua* belonging to the United Fruit Company which was torpedoed very close to George Town. After this, a Home Guard was set up to be responsible for six coastal lookouts. One of these was situated in a hut at the top of a 60-foot high silk cotton tree at Fort George on the waterfront in George Town. The hut was reached by a very long ladder.

In May 1942, the American base, codenamed **Baldpate**, was moved to a large area behind the George Town library. A wooden building with a tin roof and mosquito screens was built to serve as the barracks, mess hall and galley. Tents were used as sleeping quarters. A fuel depot, ammunition store, firing range and jetty were built at North Sound. This area was where the US seaplanes – PB Consolidated Catalinas and the larger PBM Martin Mariners landed for refuelling. These air patrols really helped to reduce the activity of enemy submarines which destroyed goods vessels. Caymanians found employment at the base and mixed with the American soldiers. On their time off, the soldiers went to Hislop's ice cream parlour and the Tea Shoppe run by Madeline and Myrtle Ebanks and the 'Petra Plantation' which is now the Grand Old House, a fine restaurant on South Church Street. In 1942, Captain Rayal Bodden's daughter Lilian married the American Chief Warrant Officer Jack Howard.

Sixty two members of the TVNVR returned home on 10 August 1945 and A C Panton, the acting Commissioner said:

'We rejoice in your safe return to the old Rock, the land of you birth, the land to which you have brought renown by reason of your conduct at the place of duty. . . . You'll always look back with pride on the fact that you wore the King's uniform when our Empire's existence was at stake.'

After the war, there was much maritime employment abroad and Caymanian seamen found work on United Fruit Company boats and National Bulk Carriers owned by Daniel K Ludwig. On this shipping line Caymanians could be trained and were promoted to high positions within the company. Some became chief engineers, while others became captains of supertankers travelling all over the world. Nearer home, there was employment in shipyards in the Belmont dry dock in Jamaica and at Cayman Boats Ltd. **Cayman Boats Ltd** was managed by Arnold 'Cappy' Foster whose clients included Errol Flynn.

In 1949, the US Government granted Caymanian seamen visa waiver, which still exists. All this employment added to the prosperity of the Cayman Islands, and funds were sent home from abroad. The widespread travelling, together with the two previous periods of migration in Caymanian history, has made for the easy acceptance of other nationalities to the islands, even though the immigration department has to be very strict. As many a captain will tell you – there isn't much of the world that they haven't seen.

1962 – CHOOSING TO BECOME A CROWN COLONY

The complex process of deciding whether to choose closer ties with Jamaica or the UK started in 1947 when the idea of a West Indies Federation was put forward to deal with the possible independence of various Caribbean islands. The Federation was finally formed in January 1958. The Cayman Islands was concerned with the method by which they would gain the most independence and control over entry to the islands, their taxation and their already flourishing overseas trade and employment. One official noted that they wished to maintain 'their virtual internal autonomy in the face of increasing self-government in Jamaica and the advent of a British Caribbean Federation . . .'.

There were two sides within the political debate led by Ducan Merren and Ormond L Panton. Interestingly, both sides wanted the same outcome; the argument was, which arrangement would give the Caymanians what they wanted. Ducan Merren represented the merchants who thought that staying with Britain was the route to local control over revenue and taxation, which would, of course, maintain his standard of living, whereas Ormond Panton, who represented the more working class on the island, believed that maintaining closer ties with Jamaica was the right route.

Ducan Merren had worked for an oil company in Louisiana before taking over the trading company his father Henry O Merren had started in 1906. In 1956, Governor Foot described the man, which also gives some insight to the trade in Cayman at the time:

'Ducan Merren is the most active member of the large Merren family which runs the biggest trading company operating in the Caymans and particularly since the war he and his many brothers have made tremendous profits. They own one of the ships which brings supplies to the Caymans and though there are one or two other traders (principally the McTaggart family) the Merrens in fact fix all retail prices in the Caymans and there is no other merchant strong enough to stand against them. The amount of profit which they obtain from their retail sales is prodigious and with so much development going on in Grand Cayman and no income tax they have been rapidly making a fortune. Amongst other enterprises they run the Pageant Beach Hotel.'

There were several Merren stores in town. Today, this area is Merren Plaza opposite the Wharf restaurant where an HSBC bank was built in 2007.

◀ The Wharf today – on the site that belonged to Ducan Merren

Conferences were held between 1959 and 1961 to which Cayman sent five delegates: Ducan Merren, Roy McTaggart, Willie Farrington, Ormond Panton and Commissioner Jack Rose. In 1961, the Jamaican Governor Kenneth Blackburne outlined ideas of how things would work when the Federation became independent. In the event, the Federation was dissolved in May 1962, just before Jamaica became an independent nation on 6 August 1962 with Norman Manley as Prime Minister.

In January 1962, Governor Blackburne attempted to put all sides of the issue fairly. The fact that he said that Britain did not rule out self government, together with the Sister Islands' almost unanimous decision to be a separate crown colony, helped the Cayman Islands make up their mind to go with Britain. It was stated by the Assembly that:

'It is the wish of the Cayman Islands:

1. To continue their present association with Her Majesty's Government in the United Kingdom.

2. To negotiate with Her Majesty's Government in the United Kingdom for the internal self-government, taking into account the wishes of the people of the Cayman Islands as to timing.'

So it was agreed that Caymanians would carry UK passports with the Cayman Islands' emblem on the front, they would fly the Union Jack and sing the British national anthem. Britain retained responsibility for defence, foreign affairs and internal security. There would be a Governor appointed by the British who would have the role of Chief Executive.

Today, royal visits are widely-celebrated events. Her Majesty the Queen and Prince Philip visited the Islands in 1983 and 1994 when she made investitures and read the speech to the Legislature. Prince Edward and Prince Andrew also visited in the 1990s and early 2000s. In 1983, The Queen opened the Queen's Highway, and in 1994 unveiled the Memorial Plaque of the Wreck of the Ten Sail – both in East End. Every year there are symbolic ceremonies such as the formal opening of the Legislature and a celebration of the Queen's Birthday Honours. There are also awards investitures at Government House and the observance of Remembrance Day.

▲ Plaque at Queen's Highway, East End

In August 1972, the Constitution was changed. This followed a report based on a month-long trip to Cayman by the Earl of Oxford and Asquith who was a constitutional expert. Now, the Legislative Assembly elected four of its members to serve on the Executive Council balanced by the **Governor** and three of his appointed officials: The **Chief Secretary**, the Governor's deputy – responsible for internal and external affairs; the **Attorney General** – responsible for legal administration and the **Financial Secretary** – responsible for finance and development. The four elected members were assigned portfolios by the Governor. These portfolios are: Health, Education and Social Services; Agriculture, Lands and Natural Resources; Communications and Works and Tourism, Aviation and Trade. The Sister Islands are represented by two members of the Assembly.

In 1991 the Constitution was reviewed but no major changes were made, apart from adding a fifth elected member (now known as ministers) and creating a more formal ministerial system, which was brought into effect in 1994. Portfolios are now called ministries if they are run by an elected member and portfolios if run by civil servants.

The Governor has responsibility for matters of defence, external affairs, internal surety, police and the civil service. The civil service has grown from about 30 in just a few departments to 3000 posts in over 60 departments and 69 authorities. There are many Caymanians in the civil service, but there are also many expatriates. The civil service includes the following departments: includes departments such as Customs, the Post Office and Treasury, education, health, the police, the central planning authority, the port authority, the mosquito research and control unit, departments of agriculture, employment, lands and survey and Radio Cayman. There are also departments of the public service commission, personnel department, the pension board and others. The expatriates working in these departments are from all over the world – so are the judges and lawyers.

THE DEVELOPMENT OF MODERN CAYMAN

There are various inextricably linked aspects of Cayman that need to be explained to understand how the Islands have developed so swiftly from the relatively rural 1970s into the sophisticated Islands they are today. Several factors needed to be addressed and developed to organise Grand Cayman into one of the top financial centres. It already had a reputation for being properly regulated and therefore safe and secure. Land had to be accurately surveyed and ownership established and registered, so that it could be sold to developers building banks and hotels, or foreign owners. Air transportation and the airport had to be upgraded to bring in the prospective investors and tourists. Telecommunications also had to come up to speed. Lastly, in order to make Cayman a place that people would want to stay to holiday or conduct business, the pesky mosquito had to be effectively controlled and hopefully completely eliminated.

▲ Cruise ship at night

FINANCIAL CENTRE

The most dynamic individuals instrumental in the Islands' financial development were retired sea captains, returned migrants and Cayman Brackers. These people sought sound advice, attracted capital and welcomed reputable people seeking residence. They proved to be good listeners and fast learners and made sure that Caymanians controlled the process of change and shared the substantial rewards from what became no less than financial alchemy. American, Canadian and British businessmen and British officials were fundamental in the building of an efficient and multi-cultural business and tourist centre. The Crown Colony status must have helped. The immigration laws have always been strict which has helped control and mould Caymanian citizenship. The Cayman Stock Exchange (CSX), founded in July 1997, was a further sign of prosperity and sophistication.

Grand Cayman was modelled on the financial centres of Bermuda and The Bahamas which had no direct taxation and a guarantee of complete privacy. The **Caymanian Bank Secrecy Law**, passed in1976, was very important as it made it illegal for a bank or officers to reveal to anyone inside or outside the islands anything about a customer's dealing with the bank.

Sir Vassel G Johnson

Sir Vassel Johnson was born in Golden Grove, Jamaica, in 1922. His parents were East Indian. They moved to the Isle of Pines when he was four years old, where they would have met Caymanians and, in 1934, his mother moved the family to Grand Cayman. Sir Vassel went to George Town Primary School and, even at this early age, he was brilliant at school. He started work in the Civil Service in 1942 as a clerk in an office of the courts. During the War he served in the local Home Guard and the Jamaican Defence Force and resumed work in the Caymanian Civil Service in 1945 as a clerical assistant in the Department of Treasury, Customs and Post Office.

▲ Sir Vassel Johnson

Sir Vassell continued working for the Civil Service for the next 30 years and built a reputation, as Craton says:

> 'for capability and forethought in financial matters, and for combining ambition and hard work with absolute integrity. In 1972 he was appointed as the first Financial Secretary, the ExCo member for Finance and Development, a post he held for 10 years. At the end of the century Sir Vassel Johnson was still on the board of the Monetary Authority'.

Sir Vassel Johnson was knighted by the Queen in 1994 and *The Caymanian Compass* wrote an article which explained that: 'He was determined to work at establishing the economic environment to create jobs for Caymanians', so 'He began to scan the horizon of the financial future of the Cayman Islands. He had a dream to create a leading offshore financial centre'.

Also involved in the creation of the centre were James McDonald who worked on the **Landmark Companies Law 1960** and William Grundy who was responsible for the **Bank and Trust Companies Law 1966**.

In 1990, Cayman had its own satellite Earth station and, by 1996, when a fibre-optic cable was laid between Grand Cayman, Cayman Brac and Jamaica, Cayman's telecommunications system was on a par with the rest of the world.

The Cayman Stock Exchange (CSX) was set up in July 1997 and included the Maverick Fund Ltd – one of the largest hedge funds in the world. In 1998, the CSX moved into the euro bond trading market.

THE DEVELOPMENT OF AIR TRANSPORTATION

Jamaica Air Transport was the first airline to fly to the Cayman Islands and was set up by King Parker Jr, who was from Tampa in the US. The service started in 1947 and flew between Kingston, Montego Bay, Grand Cayman and Cayman Brac. Ducan Merren was a shareholder. In the same year, King Parker sold the company to RAF Wing Commander Owen 'Bobby' Roberts who renamed it **Caribbean International Airlines**. By 1950, the service included Tampa and Belize.

On 10 April 1953, during the completion of a bigger airfield on Grand Cayman, Owen Roberts died when his Lodestar airline crashed on take-off from Palisadoes Airport in Kingston, Jamaica. The Cayman airfield opened in March 1954 and was named **Owen Roberts** in memory of this very likeable man. In 1968, the **Civil Aviation Authority** took over, resurfaced the runway and created **Cayman Airways** with flights between Grand Cayman, Kingston, Montego Bay and Miami. The terminal building at the Owen Roberts airfield opened in 1984.

▲ Cruise ships and roots by George Town

BEGINNING OF TOURISM

Englishman **Benson Greenall** bought land on Seven Mile Beach and built the **Galleon Beach Hotel** which had 12 rooms and opened in the winter season of 1950–51. This was a luxury hotel and stood where the **Westin Casuarina Resort** now stands. **The Caymanian Hotels Aid Law 1950** provided exemptions for import duties and taxes for anyone building a hotel with more than 10 rooms. Merren built the **Seaview Lodge** in 1952 and the **Pageant Beach Hotel**, with 36 rooms, in 1954. Benson Greenall enlarged Galleon Beach to 84 rooms in January 1956 and it was described as 'one of the finest hotel buildings in the West Indies'.

▲ The Westin Casuarina – on the site of the original Galleon Beach Hotel

The **Coral Caymanian Hotel** and three smaller hotels were built between 1957 and 1958. The **Brac Buccaneer's Inn** on Cayman Brac with 24 rooms and the **Southern Cross Club** on Little Cayman were built by 1960.

Scuba diving was introduced by **Bob Soto** in the 1970s. The **Tourism Law 1974** created the **Department of Tourism**. **Eric Bergstrom** was the first director and he had a generous budget. The **Port Authority** which improved harbour facilities and could service cruise ships and unload construction materials swiftly and efficiently was created in 1973. The **Holiday Inn**, where the **Courtyard Marriot** now stands – was, for years, one of the main hotels on Grand Cayman and had 125 rooms in the 1972–3 season. The **Barefoot Man** played there every night – he now plays twice a week at the **Reef Resort** in East End.

◀ The Barefoot Man now performs at the Reef East End, but used to play every night at the Holiday Inn

The **Anchorage Centre** in George Town was an arcade of upmarket shops for tourists. The **Palm Height** project was a 200-room hotel with 84 condominiums, a golf course and a marina, all on a 77-acre lot across the West Bay Road towards North Sound. In 1987, this became the **Hyatt Regency, Britannia Villas and golf course**. There was a condominium boom during the 1980s, which started the extensive building along Seven Mile Beach.

▲ The Hyatt

James Manoah Bodden

Known as Mr Jim, James Manoah Bodden served from 1976 to 1984 as the member of the ExCo responsible for tourism, aviation and trade. He revitalised the islands. Born in 1930 at Lower Valley, Grand Cayman, he was the son of a seaman and migrated to Port Arthur, Texas at the age of 17. He initially worked for tanker companies then settled ashore, married an American and so became a US citizen. At this point, his employment was varied and he worked as a private detective, the owner of a costume jewellery and novelty business and a taxicab company. During this time he was also general manger of a frozen foods company in Beaumont, Texas. Jim Bodden returned to Grand Cayman in 1960s with plans to start a hotel and when this did not work out he went back to sea. He started a charter boat business and a real estate company. In 1972, Mr Jim entered politics, winning the seat for Bodden Town. He was a serving member of the Legislative Assembly from 1972–88 and became a national hero only six years after his death in 1988. His statue stands in Heroes' Square bearing the inscription:

> JAMES MANOAH BODDEN MLA,
> October 5th, 1930 – May 7th, 1988
> SERVING MEMBER OF THE LEGISLATIVE ASSEMBLY
> FROM 1972 – 1988
> EXECUTIVE COUNCIL MEMBER OF
> TOURISM, AVIATION AND TRADE 1976 – 1984
> A Great Leader And Our National Hero
> "Always Loved and Remembered."

◀ Statue of James Manoah Bodden

LAND REGISTRATION

The important task of legally defining land registration began in 1971 and was completed five years later. One of the overseers of this was Bruce Campbell who still lives here and first came to the Cayman Islands after reading a job advertisement in the paper while a lawyer in the UK. This was to work with W S Walker, which was, at the time, one of the most important law firms and whose striking blue and white, classically columned building can be seen in George Town. Bruce Campbell's main work was in land registration and this was a long and complicated business. David Legge, publisher and photographer, has said

▲ Bruce Campbell

43

that William S Walker, a young Cambridge-educated lawyer arrived in Cayman with a multi-point plan to transform Grand Cayman into a world class, offshore, financial centre, so he was also instrumental in the transformation of the Islands. Proper land registration laws were very important within this plan. Financial rewards were seen as early as 1977 as the selling of lands to outsiders brought in nine times the amount of revenue than previously. David Legge reminds us in an article written in his magazine: 'These are very special individuals and their foresight and hard work arriving on an island with less than six telephones, and swarms of mosquitoes are key to how Cayman has developed today'.

Dr George Giglioni

Mosquitoes were a pest on Cayman, especially in the summer rainy season and needed to be controlled if more investors were to buy property and develop hotels. In the old days, Caymanians had tended green bush fires that kept mosquitoes away, but the smoke made people red-eyed. Dr George Giglioni was an Italian entomologist resident in British Guiana who visited Cayman with the World Health Organisation in 1948. He officially started his campaign against the mosquito in 1949. From 1951 he worked under the supervision of the Health Officer Bertie Ebanks.

His second campaign began in the late 1950s when a Todd insecticidal Fog Applicator was mounted on the back of a truck which was then driven around the Islands. This made Cayman mosquito free for 24 hours and the beneficial effects continued for several days afterwards.

The Mosquito Research and Control Unit (MRCU) was set up in January 1966 with Dr Marco E C Giglioli – George's son – as director. A Mosquito Law passed in November 1966 enabled the Unit to use any part of the Islands as an experimental control area. The work of the Unit attracted expatriate volunteers, young scientists working on doctoral theses and workers from VSO, so much research was carried out. In 1974, the Natural Resources Laboratory was set up which eventually became the Department of the Environment.

Every effort was, and still is, continually made to eradicate mosquitoes. All ships coming in to Grand Cayman and the Sister Islands were sprayed. The main breeding grounds in the swamps were sprayed to kill the larvae as well as the mature insects. Originally, DDT was used, but the authorities moved on to modern insecticides and larvicides and the efficacy of new bacterial and hormonal agents was assessed. A network of canals constructed through the mangrove swamps in Grand Cayman allowed the high tides to inundate the swamps more completely and wash away the mud in which the mosquitoes laid their eggs. This also helped the rainwater to drain into the sea more quickly, giving the larvae no time to develop into mature insects. A sprayer aircraft was introduced in 1971 and a second in 1974. These actually flew just above the roads of the Islands. In the 1970s, the number of tourists rose directly as a result of controlling the mosquito problem. Dr Marco Giglioni died in 1984, having achieved much of what he set out to do, and by 1993, mosquitoes were almost completely under control.

CAYMAN SHIELD AND THE NATIONAL SYMBOLS

The official coat of arms for the three Cayman Islands was first used in 1958. In the centre is a shield with blue and white wavy lines representing the sea. Three green stars on a gold background represent the three individual, but united, Islands. There is a lion representing the protective nature of the UK and below the shield are the words '*He hath founded it upon the Seas*' taken from Psalm 24. Above the shield is a green turtle, the creature that first attracted European visitors and which was an important mainstay of the economy for over 200 years. The turtle is standing on a coil of rope made from the leaves of the silver thatch palm unique to Cayman. A pineapple at the top represents the Cayman Islands' 300-year tie with Jamaica.

In 1993, the song 'Beloved Isle Cayman' by Leila Ross Shier was adopted as the national song. There are three national symbols – the silver thatch palm is the national tree, the wild banana orchid the national flower and the Cayman parrot the national bird.

Cayman parrot ▶

❷ Guide to Grand Cayman

GENERAL INFORMATION

Capital: George Town
Religion: Christian
Language: English

Area and population

The Cayman Islands constitutes three islands – Grand Cayman, Cayman Brac and Little Cayman – all of which are the peaks of underwater mountains situated to the south of Cuba in the Caribbean Sea. The total area is 77 square miles and the population is estimated at 60 000, of which half are Caymanian. The largest island is Grand Cayman which is about 22 miles long and eight miles at its widest point. The highest point on the Island is only 60 feet above sea level. The area of Cayman Brac is 14 square miles and Little Cayman, 10 square miles. Between the Cayman Islands and Jamaica is the Cayman Trough which is the deepest part of the Caribbean Sea at 4 miles deep. South of Cayman is the Barlett Deep which is at a depth of over 18 000 feet. All three islands are surrounded by coral reefs which lie at the top of dramatic walls and drop-offs close to the shore making it a perfect location for diving and sport fishing.

Government

The Cayman Islands is a British dependency with a British Governor appointed by the UK Government. The 15-member Legislative Assembly and the Executive Council, elected by members, is responsible for the daily administration of the country. The Governor must normally take the advice of the council, except in matters of defence, internal security, external affairs, police and civil service.

Airlines

The main scheduled airlines that fly into Grand Cayman are: Spirit, Cayman Airways, Continental, Delta, Northwest, US Airways, American Airlines, British Airways, Air Canada, Air Jamaica and Atlantic Airlines Northwest. Cayman Airways operates daily flights between Grand Cayman and the Sister Islands. Island Air offers domestic and international charters and Cayman Helicopters also offers charters.

Climate

Temperatures are at their lowest in February, ranging from 60°– 86° F maximum in July. The humidity is 68–92 per cent. Rainfall is seasonal and varies over the islands. Eastern districts tend to be drier and Cayman Brac has less rain than Grand Cayman. The rainy season starts in May and the maximum rainfall is in September and October. You can read a weather forecast in the local daily newspaper *The Caymanian Compass* and on the website www.caycompass.com

Driving

Drive on the left and wear a seatbelt. You need a visitor's driving licence from a car rental agency or from the vehicle and driving licensing department next to the central police station in George Town. Just show your valid driving licence from your country of residence and pay the fee.

Drugs

Zero tolerance. If you are found with a small quantity of marijuana this is usually met with a fine of several hundred dollars. Possession of cocaine, ecstasy etc has, in some cases, resulted in prison sentences.

Money and banking

Banking hours are from 09.00–16.00 Monday to Thursday and until 16.40 on Fridays. The CI dollar is issued in CI$100, 50, 25, 10, 5 and 1 denominations and coins are 25, 10, 5 and 1 cent. US dollars are accepted island wide, but expect your change in CI dollars. ATM machines are available island wide.

Public transport

The main taxi rank is in the centre of George Town, but taxis can be hailed on most of the busy roads. Taxi companies also act as tour operators, so can show you around the island. The bus depot is next to the library in central George Town. The bus route covers West Bay, Seven Mile Beach, Bodden Town, North Side and East End areas.

There are five main routes, each marked with a different coloured circle: West Bay to Turtle Farm – yellow; West Bay to Birch Tree Hill – green; Bodden Town – blue; East End – red; North Side – orange (extended on request to Rum Point). Call the Public Transport Hotline, tel 345 945 5100 for the daily schedule.

Radio and television

Cayman has 13 FM radio stations catering for all musical tastes. **Radio Cayman 1** (89.9 MHz in Grand Cayman and 93.9 MHz in the Sister Islands) and **Breeze FM** (105.3 MHz in Grand Cayman and 91.9 MHz in the Sister Islands) are government owned; **Cayrock** (96.5 MHz) – classic and contemporary rock music; **z99** (99.9 MHz) – top 40 music 24 hours a day; **Vibe** (98.9 MHz) local and reggae music; **Spin** (94.9 MHz) – rhythm and blues, calypso; **Rooster** (101.9 MHz) – country and western; **Hot** (104.1 MHz) – reggae, soca and rhythm and blues; **Kiss** (106.1 MHz) – golden oldies; 107.9 MHz broadcasts the government weather information. Local television stations: **CITN** (Cayman Islands Television Network); **CCT** (Cayman Christian Television) and **Westar TV** US cable television is available island wide.

Telecommunications

Cable and Wireless and **Digicel**. Cable and Wireless internet hot spots are located throughout the islands.

Time

Time is Eastern Standard Time and does not observe daylight saving.

Working and immigration

As these islands are very small, a strict immigration policy is in place – anyone found overstaying or working without a permit is likely to face deportation. To obtain a work permit you have to first find a job

▲ Immigration Department, George Town

and the company employing you will file for the work permit. The Cayman Islands has more jobs than there are people on the islands to fill the positions. Preference, of course, is given to Caymanians who are properly qualified for the job.

Magazines

Key to Cayman, www.keytocayman.com

Horizons, the magazine of Cayman Airways is published bi-monthly and is an excellent, up-to-date guide to the Cayman Islands.

Grand Cayman, edited by David Legge, is a very glossy quarterly magazine. It has a very high standard of articles and photography, and is a showcase of excellence in the Cayman Islands. It also is the *Hello*, *OK* and *Tatler* of the Cayman Islands, with society pictures covering all the glittering parties and dinners and charity events.

Emergency phone numbers
Police/fire/ambulance: 911
Dentist: 945 4388
Decompression Chamber: 555
Hyperbolic Chamber: 949 2989
Red Cross: 949 6785

Taxis
AAA Yellow Cab: 444 4444
Ace Taxi & Tour Service: 777 7777
Charlie's Super Cab & Tours: 888 8888
Taxi Service & Tours: 949 5702

Government phone numbers
Administrative building: 949 7900
Customs: 949 2473
Immigration: 949 8344
Port Authority: 949 2055
Post Office: 949 2474
Library: 949 5159
Tourism: 949 0623
Directory Enquiries: 411
Chamber of Commerce: 949 8090

Cayman Airways: 949 2311
Cayman Islands Tourist Board: www.caymanislands.ky or www.divecayman.ky

Car hire

Go to **Avis**, avisgcm@candw.ky, whose offices are right across from the airport for Honda Civics, the fabulous convertible PT Cruiser or a Jeep.

▲ Convertible PT Cruiser from Avis

The National Trust of the Caymans

Founded in 1987 by the National Trust for the Cayman Islands Law, this is responsible for the preservation of the natural, maritime and historic heritage of the Cayman Islands. The Trust's properties and sites include:

Grand Cayman
Bodden Town Guard House Park
East End Lighthouse Park
Fort George
Governor Michael Gore Bird Sanctuary
Heritage Beach (East End)
Mastic Reserve and Mastic Trail
Miss Izzy's School House
Queen Elizabeth II Botanic Park
Salina Reserve
Trust House
Mission House
Watlers Cemetery

Cayman Brac
Cayman Brac Parrot Reserve and Nature Trail

Little Cayman
Booby Pond Nature Reserve

▲ Female Blue Iguana

▲ Mission House, Bodden Town

▲ Lake at Queen Elizabeth II Botanic Park

If you manage to visit all these attractions, then you will have properly experienced the heritage of the Cayman Islands. You can pick up a map and start your tour or visit their website www.caymannationaltrust.org, tel 949 0121, email: ntrust@candw.ky.

You can also become a member of the Trust if you live on the island or live abroad and are interested in the Cayman's heritage. The Trust depends on the support of its members, their membership fees and donations.

Main areas of Grand Cayman

WEST BAY

Starting south of the Governor's residence, West Bay is one of the oldest and most characterful areas. It has been inhabited for over 200 years and so has much charm and character. Boggy Sand Road (turn left at the fourway stop) is a mixture of traditional architecture and multimillion-dollar homes. There are cottages here that were fishermen's cottages and date back to 1910. Places to visit here are Boatswain's Beach, the Turtle Farm, Morgan's Harbour, Hell, Hell Post Office and Barkers National Park which covers 276 acres of low lying coast and wetland and 865 acres of protected marine habitat with coral reefs and offshore habitats for marine turtles and lobster. The seagrass beds encourage conch and small turtles. Green and loggerhead sea turtles find nesting sites on Barkers' completely unspoilt beaches. Local and migratory birds find nesting and feeding grounds inland. A walking tour of the wetlands is a must as it is very peaceful. The beaches are great for kite surfing and lessons can be organised here.

▲ Shell stall

▲ Church and Town Hall, West Bay

GEORGE TOWN

George Town is home to 500 banks and 300 insurance companies, not to mention lawyers, accountants and hedge fund companies, so business is brisk. Harbour Drive, the road along the waterfront is a tourist's haven. There is a National Trust walking tour of George Town that takes you around the oldest buildings. These include the ruins of Fort George (1739), the National Museum (1833) at the Harbour, the Peace Memorial (1919), Elmslie Memorial Church (1922), and the Library and Post Office (1939). Heroes' Square is flanked by the clean white lines of the Law Courts and Government Building and has beautiful fountains in the centre as well as the James Bodden statue, the Mariners' Memorial – a beautiful sculpture of two men at sea; and black marble plaques listing the names of national heroes. Also worth looking at, situated down the road on the side of the Law Courts, is John Broad's mural depicting 500 years of Cayman history. It is a beautifully painted mural on 500 tiles organised into pictures of the main milestones in Cayman's history. Contact the Tourist Board for the latest times of walks around George Town organised by the National Trust when you can learn more history and the reasons behind road names.

▲ George Town Harbour

▲ Margaritaville, Breezes and shops on George Town waterfront

▲ Cruise ships

SPEEDWAY PUBLIC LIBRARY
SPEEDWAY, INDIANA

▲ Fort George

The library in George Town was constructed between 1937 and 1939 and officially opened it doors to the public in 1940. It was built by **Captain Rayal B Bodden**, MBE JP who built Cayman's first motorised ship the *Cimboco* and the *Lady Slater* which was one of the largest motor vessels ever built in Cayman. Bodden's shipbuilding excellence can be seen in the design of the library as its ceiling looks like a ship's hull. It suffered major roof damage during Hurricane Ivan and 10 000 books were lost. It has now been repaired and restored.

▲ Fountains in Heroes' Square

BODDEN TOWN

Bodden Town takes its name from the first residents – the Boddens. Originally, it was the capital of the Cayman Islands as it had good vantage points looking out to sea, and a good harbour suitable for large sailing ships. It was also originally called 'Southside' or 'Old Isaacs'. Some of the most fertile soil in the island can be found nearby in Newlands and Lower Valley, which was another reason for its early habitation. Over the years, hurricanes have changed the channels so that now only small boats can operate from here. The seat of government and the capital moved to George Town in the early 1900s.

William Bodden was one of the most prominent early Caymanians who lived here. He was Governor from 1773 with a commission as magistrate from Governor Balearees (Jamaica) in 1798. He served as Chief Magistrate or 'Custos' until his death in 1823.

▲ The Guard House

The **Guard House** is a small square building at the western entrance to Bodden Town, on the bend of the road, with a thatched roof and cannons outside. This dates from the 1830s (but is a replica) and stands on a slight hill known as **Guard House Hill**. It was once the town's defensive outpost against pirates and Spanish marauders and was manned by the local militia armed with cannons, muskets and swords.

Just around the corner, marked by two eighteenth-century cannons pointing downwards (a recognised, worldwide, nautical tradition), was the other defence point as it overlooked one of the principal channels. The open space across the road, facing the sea, provided a clear line of cannon fire to repel would-be invaders attempting to enter the channel. For many years, one of the cannons lay buried in the sand until it was dug out in 1910 by four men – Henry Bodden, Procklington McCoy, Conwell Solomon and Thomas Tatum and placed in the position seen today. They also built two benches near the cannons on which people may sit and look out to sea.

Gun Square ▶

Down this road marked by the cannons is the **Mission House**, a Cayman National Trust house which is open every day in the winter months and every morning during the quieter, summer months.

There is a monument to Queen Victoria in the town which was built when Sir Sydney Olivier was Governor of Jamaica and George Hirst Commissioner of Cayman Islands (1907–12). In the 1920s and 30s, the monument was a regular meeting site for the men of Bodden Town to discuss local politics – a tradition that still continues today.

Meagre Bay Pond is just east of Bodden Town and was shown on an early map of Cayman in 1773 as Mauger Bay. A later map, drawn in 1881, first showed it as Meagre Pond. In 1910, Hirst reported it as a hunting and shooting ground for teal and mallard. Both were hunted to near extinction but recently have returned and it is now an animal sanctuary and nature reserve. This is a favourite spot for bird-watchers as there are many snowy egrets. The pond is part of the central mangrove that drains into the North Sound, but tidal fluctuation rarely reaches this far inland.

Pirates' Caves are a series of vast underground caverns, which are very warm and said to be the caves where pirates of old hid their treasure. They certainly have a strange atmosphere and pirate artefacts such as treasure chests, skeletons, lanterns and some stocks are on display. You are given a torch to explore the darker areas. Look out for the foot sticking out of the cave wall. You may also spot bats down here. Above ground there is a small farm, which has an iguana, parrots, pigs, horses, donkeys, ducks and a stingray.

 Pirate caves

BREAKERS

Breakers is named after the white waves commonly seen off the coast. This is where the Barefoot Man has his home on one of the white sandy beaches looking out over the Caribbean Sea. Breakers is truly Caymanian and very unspoilt. You drive along the most beautiful, wide open coastline. Don't miss a visit to the **Lighthouse Restaurant** which is one of the best Italian restaurants on the island – it has a fantastic view.

Lighthouse Restaurant ▶

EAST END

Here you can find true Caymanian living and unspoilt beaches. Here are traditional cottages, small stores and bars. There are also many churches. **Blow Holes** is on the coast and is so-called because sea water is forced through holes in the ironshore to create natural geyser-like fountains. Since Hurricane Ivan in 2004, the fountains do not rise as high. Here are also many old shipwrecks that came to grief on the treacherous sharp coral reefs. **Wreck of the Ten Sails Park** is where the legendary shipwreck described on page 13 took place in 1794. The wreck area can be viewed from the lighthouse built by the British Government in 1937 and there is a memorial plaque looking over the site, which was

unveiled by the Queen in 1994. There is an older lighthouse nearby. The main road leading from East End to Old Man Bay is called the **Queen's Highway** and was opened by Queen Elizabeth II in February 1983.

◀ Blow Holes

NORTH SIDE

This was the last district to be settled and another area where true traditional Caymanian life can be experienced. The earliest residents were freed slaves in search of unclaimed land. It was isolated from the rest of the island due to its lack of roads and only ironshore to traverse. The older generation hardly ever made trips to town. Electricity and telephones only arrived in the 1970s. This trip now only takes 40 minutes along excellent roads!

North Side can be reached by taking a left turn as you are coming from George Town at Frank Sound, or you can take the long, scenic way around by going straight ahead via East End and the Queen's Highway which eventually brings you to Old Man Bay. There is a craft shop here and a grocery store on your right, by the playing fields. In North Side you can visit the **Queen Elizabeth II Botanical Park** and walk the **Mastic Trail**, which follows the original cross-island trails dating back to the 1700s. **Cayman Kai** on the very tip of North Side peninsula has beautiful, huge homes and holiday villas, the Kaibo Bar and Grill and great beaches. **Rum Point** is a must for snorkelling and relaxing in hammocks by the beach where the water is waist deep until very far out. It is great for children! You can take a boat trip to Rum Point from town and many boats moor up here at the weekend for parties.

▲ Queen Elizabeth II Botanic Garden

Beaches

Seven Mile Beach

Anywhere on this fabulous stretch of white sand and clear, turquoise water is perfect. Nothing, however, prepares you for the absolute intensity of the colour of the sea. Some parts of the beach are in front of the big hotels or condominium developments, but all is public – you just can't use the beach chairs unless you are resident, so take a towel. Most people go to one of the many places listed below.

▲ Seven Mile Beach

Governors Beach – just in front of the Governor's House.

Public Beach – on the West Bay Road, two miles from Governors Beach. This has an excellent playground, cabanas and picnic tables for barbeques, restrooms and showers

◀ Playground at West Bay Public Beach

Cemetery Beach – further north, towards West Bay. Park by the cemetery and enter the beach by way of the signposted path. Try the beach by Calico Jack's or Royal Palms for lunch

Rum Point – right beyond North Side on the furthest tip of the island from West Bay. You can either drive or catch a ferry from the Hyatt in George Town or charter a boat or yacht and bring a picnic here. Here is the perfect place to relax. There is the most wonderful beach with shallow water for miles, so children absolutely love it. There is a very long dock which is great to walk along and take in all that horizon and turquoise sea and azure sky. Red Sail Sports has a shop here where you can book diving, snorkelling, boat, jet ski and other excursions. **The Wreck Bar** is the main bar and restaurant here and serves the best cocktails and food – fish and chips burgers salads. The waiters and waitresses are always very busy – there is a sign 'Do not feed or touch the bartenders' – good advice! And a blackboard displays questions not to ask. You have been warned!

> Do you live here? No we jet ski from Miami daily!
> Can I get US change back? Toto we are not in Kansas anymore!
> Can you swim under the island? Yeah, but please pay your toll first!
> Where is the best place to snorkel? Try the water!
> Is that Cuba on the horizon? We wish! It's only West Bay!
> Does Alpha the parrot bite? Anyone, anytime and any finger!
> How much for a virgin Mudslide? Cups of ice are free!
> Do you guys sell rum here? WELCOME TO RUM POINT!

▲ Boats at the dock Rum Point

▲ In a hammock

Smith Cove – south of George Town Harbour on South Church Street. This has picnic tables, restrooms and showers.

Spotts Beach – has cabanas, picnic tables, lounge chairs and playgrounds. The entrance and parking is next to the cemetery, past Red Bay and Prospect.

▲ Smith Cove

South Sound – reached by a drive through George Town, down the South Sound road. The entrance is between South Sound cemetery and Emerald Beach condominiums.

Barker's – in West Bay, this is secluded and great for nature walks. Drive to West Bay and follow the signs to the Pappagallo restaurant. Drive past the restaurant, through the signs and stop where you wish. It is great for kitesurfing here.

▲ Rum Point Beach

East End – stretches of deserted, unspoilt beach. Just outside Pirates' Cove Bar is a volleyball net and some beach chairs.

▲ East End Beach

Breakers – at Frank Sound, lies east along the coast road. Frank Sound Beach is on the right, just as you reach the turn off to North Side.

There are, of course many more beaches as you drive around the island just stop where you see cabanas. The locals have their favourite secret beaches which are reached by small paths between the sea grape trees.

Parks

The main Parks are Scholar's Park in West Bay, George Dixon Park in East End, Jarold Smith Park in North Side, Dart Family Park in George Town and the Airport Park. These all have well equipped playgrounds for children, some with stunning sea views.

▲ George Dixon Park, East End

Main attractions

QUEEN ELIZABETH II BOTANIC PARK

The Queen officially opened these gardens in 1994. The 65-acre park has a visitors and **Information Centre** and a wide variety of gardens to explore such as the blue iguana habitat; the **Woodland Trail** which takes 35 minutes to walk and where, occasionally, a blue iguana will cross your path, and the **Heritage Garden** – with a traditional Caymanian house at its centre and a sand garden celebrating early Caymanian life, in which grow crops such as: cassava, breadfruit and sweet potatoes; fruit trees such as mango, june plum and sweetsop; and medicinal plants such as cerasee and aloe vera. Four elderly Caymanian gardeners advised the park during its creation so that it is historically correct. The **Colour Garden** is a tropical paradise with plants in different colour areas. Here you can see bougainvillea trees,

▲ Heritage Garden

▲ Colour Garden

purple queen, sky blue plumbago flowers, red ixoras, cycads, bird of paradise, banana trees and bamboo. There is also an extensive **Lake and Wetland** area. The lake is great for bird-watchers. The Park, tel 947 9462, is open daily 09.00–18.30, April–September and 09.00–17.30, October–March. Last admission is one hour before closing. It is closed on Good Friday and Christmas Day.

▲ Iguana habitat

Boatswains' Beach Adventure Marine Park and Turtle Farm
This is home to 11 000 green sea turtles ranging in size from 6oz to 600lbs each. The farm breeds the green sea turtle and exhibits loggerhead, kemps, ridley and hawksbill turtles. There is a **research and educational facility** focusing on the conservation of sea turtles. The

farm releases some of the turtles annually in November. For information, contact tel 345 949 3894 or info@boatswainsbeach.ky.

It takes between 15 and 30 years for a green sea turtle to reach maturity and they may live to be 100 years old. At nesting time, the females will travel thousands of miles to the beach of their birth to lay eggs. The eggs will hatch 50–60 days after they are laid. Only female sea turtles come ashore to nest. Male sea turtles rarely return to land after crawling to the sea as baby turtles. The adult green sea turtle can stay under water for 12 hours while sleeping. There are tanks at the farm showing every stage of a turtle's growth. If you come between May and July you can see the baby turtles hatching from the eggs, which are laid and collected from a man-made beach within the farm. There are **touch tanks** where you can pick up the baby turtles and be photographed with them.

Boatswain's Beach (pronounced bo'suns) has **Breakers Freshwater Lagoon** which has waterfalls and a shallow end for toddlers. There is an **Iguana Hut** with a three foot Caiman – a member of the crocodile family and how the islands got their name. The **Predator Tank** has several sharks which can be seen underwater from the freshwater pool; and the **Snorkel Lagoon** which has many varieties of fish. There is also an **aviary** with the Cayman parrot and white and red ibis among very many other varieties of bird; a **Nature Trail** with examples of all the indigenous Caymanian plants including the national tree, the **Silver Thatch**, which is very slow growing and takes 300 years to grow to a height of about 3 metres (10 feet); and what is known as the **Tourist Tree** which can be recognised by its red and peeling bark. There is a blue hole (or sink hole) here which has been dated back 10 000 years – evidenced by the fossils of turtle bones. In the past, there was sea water in the hole and natives gathered around, set up camp and ate turtle.

The **Education Centre** has large, flat screen televisions, interactive computers for children and big, soft, turtle-shaped cushions. Next to this is the **Hatchery** which can be viewed through a glass wall. Turtle eggs are collected in May and put in Styrofoam boxes with sand in the bottom and cloth on top. The boxes are labelled with the date of laying and the approximate date of hatching. After 50–60 days, the eggs are removed from the boxes and laid in a shallow sandpit. In the wild, the turtle eggs would be buried much deeper in the sand – the depth being determined by the length of the mother turtle's flippers which she uses to dig the nest hole. In other words, the bigger the turtle, the deeper the hole. In the wild, the baby turtles take some time to dig themselves out of the hole so are born with a yolk sac on their tummies to live off. In the hatchery they do not have to dig themselves out and are put into a shallow water tank where the sac is absorbed in about five days. At this point they are split up into display turtles and meat production turtles. About 10 per cent are released into the wild and the rest are kept for breeding. Mating begins in March/April. The first eggs appear in May and are laid in a specially made beach near the main turtle pool. Hatching starts in July, so this is the best time to visit the farm as tiny turtles can be seen hatching from the shallow sandpits.

There is a **Caymanian street** with musicians and craftsman. You can find refreshments at **Breakers Snack Shack**, by the freshwater lagoon or lunch at **Schooners** which has great food and is also brilliant for kids' parties. The Park is open seven days a week from 08.30 to 16.30 – it is a good idea to get there early and spend the whole day there. There is a discount for Cayman residents

▲ Touch tanks

▲ Adult turtles

▲ Woodland Trail

▲ Ibis in the Aviary

▲ Breakers Freshwater Lagoon

BUTTERFLY FARM

The farm, tel 946 3411, houses 1200 butterflies of 34 different species, none of which are native to Cayman. A guide shows the phases of metamorphosis from egg to caterpillar to butterfly. Open daily 08.30–16.00.

▲ Guide

PEDRO ST JAMES

This house is known as the **birthplace of democracy** and was built in 1780 by **William Eden** as his home. In its time, it has been a home, a courthouse, a jail, the home of the government assembly, a picnic area and a restaurant.

▲ Caboose

▲ Dining room

Great Pedro was a courthouse from 1823 until 1839. It was here on 5 December 1831 that the decision was made to form the first electoral parliament in the Cayman Islands. Parliament met here for 30 years. In May 1835, the abolition of slavery was proclaimed from the top of the steps.

William Eden died in the 1850s and his family stayed on, but when his granddaughter Mary Jane Eden was killed by lightening in 1877 as she stood on the steps, the property was abandoned and fell into disrepair. The family moved

▲ Verandah and view

back in after a bad hurricane and continued to live there from 1909 until 1920. In 1954, an ex-US air force pilot and diving and tourism pioneer, Thomas Hubbell, purchased the property and repaired it. First he lived in it and then leased it as a restaurant and hotel from 1967 to 1970 and then it burned down. It was repaired and opened again as a restaurant, but burnt down again in the 1980s. The building was thought to be cursed and was left as a ruin.

The Cayman Islands' Government bought Pedro in 1991 to return it to an historic site. The great house has now been restored using authentic materials and furniture. The work was completed in 1998, but was repaired again after Hurricane Ivan. The restored great house, typical of those built between 1820 and 1840 has three levels, is open on all sides for air flow and has an outdoor kitchen or 'caboose' for cooking. The second floor was used for dining, entertaining or relaxing on the shaded verandahs. The bedrooms were on the top floor. There is a multi-media theatre, where you can see a 20-minute video that describes the history of the area. There is also a gift shop and a restaurant. Pedro Castle was built overlooking the sea on a cliff, in seven acres of landscaped grounds. A 150 year-old tree that was blown over by Hurricane Ivan has been made into a place to sit and admire the views. Here you can take time to imagine what it was like to live on an early nineteenth century West Indian plantation. Open daily 09.00–17.00.

HELL AND HELL POST OFFICE

'Hell' on Grand Cayman is a large area of blackened limestone and dolomite. The ironshore is black from the acid-secreting algae which covers the surface. There is decking around the ironshore where you can have your picture taken with the carved wooden devil. Ivan Farrington owns the gift shop and is always fabulously dressed as

a devil. He asks everyone where the hell they are from and who the hell they are. He, in fact, was a merchant seaman and will tell you that he has been to hell and back. You can send a postcard home with a hell post mark from the **Hell Post Office** next door.

◀ Ivan Farrington in devil costume

CAYMAN ISLANDS NATIONAL MUSEUM

The museum, tel 949 8368, was extensively damaged by Hurricane Ivan in 2004 and is now restored and newly open. The building, was the Old Courts on the harbour front in George Town. It was turned into a museum in 1991.

▲ The National Museum

Until Ivan, the Museum housed two permanent, and various rotating exhibitions. The **natural history exhibit** showed Cayman's varied habitats with displays of corals and limestone rocks. It had a bathymetric map which was a 3-D depiction of the undersea mountains and canyons that surround the Cayman Islands. Upstairs, was the **cultural history exhibit**, which included artefacts from domestic life and past industries such as shipbuilding, thatch rope-making, weaving and turtling. These exhibits, including coins, rare documents and a catboat, had been collected by Mr Ira Thompson since the 1930s and were purchased by the government in 1979. There were stories of fishing and the 1932 storm. All this showed how Caymanians survived in the early days with little outside contact.

The art gallery had exhibits of the group of Caymanian visual artists known as the Native Sons and displayed examples of local furniture. There was also a children's gallery with interactive displays about Cayman's heritage. All this is due to reopen in a newly renovated interior. Call tel 949 8368 or look at www.museum.ky for updates.

MARITIME HISTORY TRAILS

These are organised by a joint group including the National Museum, the National Archive, the Department of the Environment and the National Trust of the Cayman Islands. There is a poster which serves as a guide to all the maritime history spots on the Island. Noticeable signs mark places of public access where trail explorers can look out to sea at a shipwreck site, see remains of an historic fort, or an example of maritime architecture. There is a trail for Grand Cayman and another for the Sister Islands. The lighthouses on all three islands are on the trail. Maritime industries – turtling, shipbuilding and wrecking are all explained.

▲ Hog Sty Bay maritime history trail sign

BLUE DRAGON TRAIL

Scattered over the island is an outdoor art exhibit of 15 painted iguanas (also known as blue dragons). All of them have different names and colourful, decorated skins and were each created by a local artist. These can be found from Hell Road in West Bay to Rum Point in North Side. There is a map available showing where the sculptures are. The blue iguana is Grand Cayman's largest native land animal and is a dragon-like blue lizard which grows to over 1.5 metres (5 feet) long and over 25lbs in weight. Its lifespan is 60 years or more. Blue iguanas need plants, flowers and fruit to eat and shelter and soil to dig their nests.

The National Trust for the Cayman Islands began captive breeding in 1990, when wild iguanas were near extinction. Their goal is to restore 1000 of them to the wild. The captive programme holds 200 iguanas. So far, 30 have been released into the Botanic Park and 23 more into the National Trust's Salina Reserve. At the Queen Elizabeth II Botanic Park you can tour the breeding enclosures and see some 60 year-old adults, as well as babies. For more details look at www.blueiguana.ky or call the National Trust on tel 949 0121, or Blue Dragon Safaris on tel 949 0121.

▲ Iguana opposite the Post Office in George Town

▲ Iguana in South Church Street, George Town

▲ Iguana by West Bay Dock

BIRDS

The Cayman Islands are a bird-watcher's paradise with many species to be seen in peaceful and unspoilt surroundings. *Birds of the Cayman Islands* by Patricia Bradley, with photographs by Yves-Jacques Rey-Millet, has an introduction by the Duke of Edinburgh and is the best guide for the enthusiast. It includes photos of all the species to be found, including brown and red footed boobies, frigate birds, herons egrets, whistling ducks, stilts, terns doves, parrots, owls, loggerhead kingbirds, warblers, bananaquits, bullfinches, woodpeckers and grackles. The past Governor of the Cayman Islands, Michael Gore, was a keen photographer of the birdlife of the islands.

THE PHILATELLIC BUREAU

There is a bureau at the Central Post Office in George Town and also one at Seven Mile Beach Post Office in West Shore Centre on West Bay Road, tel 946 4757. Don't forget to visit the Post Office at Hell where your postcards can be franked with the special Hell postmark.

CAYMAN CAR MUSEUM

The museum is due to open in 2009 in West Bay – look out for this Andreas Ugland development housing one of the largest car museums in the world.

Galleries and artists

The **National Gallery of the Cayman** Islands, tel 945 8111, is on the ground floor of Harbour Place, South Church Street in George Town. The Gallery was established in 1996 and is an educational, non-profit-making organisation. **Nancy Barnard** is its Director and **David Bridgeman** is the Curator. The Gallery holds an average of eight exhibitions of the work of both local and international artists per year. There are also artists' workshops, lectures and annual events. The National Gallery of the Cayman Islands serves to promote and encourage the appreciation and practice of the visual arts in the Cayman Islands. Funds are being raised at present – with a goal of $2.5 million dollars – to build a new National Gallery building on the bypass. Building is planned to start in early 2008, just off the **Esterley Tibbetts Highway** near the Harquail Theatre. The chief architect and project manager is **Danny Owens** of OA&D Architects and the National Gallery Board Building Chairperson is **John Doak**, also an established architect on Grand Cayman. The new building will feature a gallery and an educational centre.

The **Kennedy Gallery**, tel 949 8077, in the West Shore Centre on the West Bay Road is owned by Joe Imperato who also owns the excellent Caribbean Club. This gallery features local artists **Miguel Powery** and **Joanne Sibley**.

The **Morgan Gallery**, Galleria Plaza, tel 943 5566, exhibits the work of various artists including Carol Owen, wife of the former Governor John Owen, Randy Chollette, Nasaria Suckoo-Chollette, Gordon Solomon, Avril Ward, April Bending and John Broad.

▲ Randy Chollette

▲ Pure Art Gallery

Pure Art, South Church Street, tel 949 9133, is housed in a beautiful, traditional, Caymanian cottage owned by Debbie van der Bol who has been in Cayman for 20 years and who is, herself, a brilliant artist. Pure Art features many local artists and also sells Caribbean gifts and crafts.

The work of **Eleanor Chalfen** www.muraka.com hangs in a number of exclusive residences on Grand Cayman and can be seen at the very chic **Luca** restaurant at the Caribbean Club on West Bay Road, in the private lounge at the **Water's Edge** condominiums and **International**

Design Group (IDG) in Seven Mile Shops on West Bay Road. Eleanor produces the most stunning abstract, close-up photographs of underwater fish and coral, uniquely capturing the essence of the amazing underwater life of Cayman. These are printed onto canvas or on photographic paper mounted behind a floating frame. Eleanor is keen to get the image right 'in camera' and spends a significant time examining her subject to find the angle that most intrigues her. Where a shot is to convey movement she will watch the subject closely and wait for the repetition of the movement that she wishes to capture. Her print runs are small – usually about 20 – and are for private sale, so they are very collectable pieces.

The work of Eleanor Chalfen ▶

Al Ebank's Studio and Gallery, George Town, tel 916 0063, is part of the Native Sons group established in 1996 to develop and promote Caymanian artists. His studio is to be found behind Phillips' electrical store at 166 Shedden Road.

A **Glass Blowing Workshop** is to be found right between McArthur's grocery store and Burger King on the waterfront on North Church Street. Here you can see the glass actually being blown and then buy from a selection of pieces.

◀ Glass blowing

Cathy Church's Underwater Photographic Centre and Gallery, tel 949 7415. Cathy is married to Herb Rafael, also a photographer. Look out for her book *My Underwater Journey* which showcases her fabulous pictures.

The **Ritz Carlton Gallery**, tel 943 9000, is located in the walkway over West Bay Road, and houses regularly changing exhibitions co-ordinated by Cayman Traditional Arts. All artwork on display is for sale.

The **Guy Harvey Gallery**, 49 South Church Street, tel 943 4891, houses original paintings, art prints and sculptures of marine life which is very popular all over the Caribbean. Guy Harvey, himself, is an eminent marine biologist, conservationist and artist and can be found painting in the store most days from 10.00 to 16.00.

Guy Harvey Gallery ▶

Island Art and Framing, tel 947 2606, is located next to the restaurant Black Pearl Galley and the surf park Grand Harbour.

Nas Art Gallery, tel: 945 8278, is the studio of **Luelen 'Luts' Bodden** which he transformed from Palm Dale into an Egyptian palace. The gallery has a painted mosaic floor, sculptural walls and alcoves that display Luts' art work. His iguana on the Blue Dragon Trail is outside Harbour Place on Harbour Drive, George Town .

The **Nelson Gallery**, tel 324 5700, at the Treasure Island resort displays Cuban art and, each month, the work of different local artists.

The **24K-Mon Jeweller and Art Gallery**, Buckingham Square, West Bay Road, tel 949 1499, stocks sculptures made from bronze, porcelain, acrylic and glass and photographs of historic Cayman. There are paintings by **April Bending, Lorna Griggs, Debbie Tibbetts-Husted, Sue Widmer, Guy Harvey** and **Lois Brezinski.**

▲ Work by April Bending

Look out for the work of other artists **Wray Banker**, **Horatio Esteban** and **David Bridgeman**.

The **McCoy Prize** in 2006/2007 was won by **Nasaria Suckoo Cholette** for her painting 'Maiden Plumb' – a bold choice. The year before, the prize went to **Nicola McCoy**. This is an important art prize on the Islands and influences art buyers.

◀ Work by Wray Banker

'Maiden Plumb' by ▶
Nasaria Suckoo-Cholette

THE CAYMAN NATIONAL CULTURAL FOUNDATION

The CNCF is a non-profit-making organisation that is funded by an annual government grant through the Ministry of Education, Human Resources and Culture as well as by contributions from private enterprise and individuals. The foundation exists to 'stimulate, facilitate and preserve the cultural and artistic expression generally, particularly the preservation and exploration of Caymanian performing, visual and literary arts'. Their Director is **Henry Muttoo**. They run **Cayfest** and **Gimistory** (see Festivals, page 76) and the hit comedy **'Rundown'** by Dave Martins directed by Henry Muttoo which is shown at the Harquail Theatre each February/March. 'Rundown' pokes fun at the Caymanian way of life, and satirises the latest politics and news. The CNCF organises shows from groups such as the **Jamaican Folk Singers** and the **Randy James Dance Works** from New Jersey. The foundation owns 101 works by

the artist **Gladwyn 'Lassie' Bush MBE** which are exhibited from time to time, and they also published a book celebrating her work: *My Markings...the art of Gladwyn K. Bush*. 'Miss Lassie', as she is affectionately known, is referred to as a fourth-generation Caymanian who began her visionary painting at the age of 62. She painted on canvas and on the walls, shutters and furnishings of her home, which still stands where Walkers Road meets South Church Street.

▲ Miss Lassie

The **Harquail Theatre** is a US$4 million facility built for the people of the Cayman Islands with funds from Mrs Helen Harquail. The building was designed by John Doak. The theatre is managed by the

CNCF and musicals, comedies and drams are regularly produced. This is where 'Rundown' is shown and the theatre has produced **pantomimes** by the Nobel Prize winning author **Derek Walcott**. Productions of **Frank McField's** plays including *Playground* have also been staged here.

▲ The Harquail Theatre

The CNCF has published **Grown From This Ground**, a book of poetry by Leonard Dilbert; **Smoke-Pot Days**, a book of memoirs by Caymanian folk historian, Mr Percival 'Will' Jackson and **Downside Up** and **Time Longer dan Rope**, two plays by the playwright Frank McField. They have produced audiotapes of the late Mr Radley Gourzong performing traditional Caymanian fiddle music with the Happy Boys and of the Caymanian singer/guitarist Roy Bodden performing country and western standards. They have also published CD and video performances of 'Aunt' Julia Hydes and Mr Septimore Scott.

The CNCF runs many workshops in dance, choral singing, oil painting, fabric dyeing, ceramics, stage lighting, poetry, playwriting and theatre. Young at Arts is their youth arts company providing training in theatre and dance.

FESTIVALS

Agricultural Show – February

2008 will see the forty-first annual Agricultural Show which is held at the Agricultural Pavilion in Savannah. The opening is marked by horses with riders holding flags which they pass over to members of the cadet corps in front of the main stage. The British and Cayman National Anthems are sung and prominent members of the

▲ Traditional Cayman band

Government and the Governor attend. There are 22 entry categories for every kind of vegetable, livestock and arts and crafts on Grand Cayman and all entries are judged and prizes awarded. Besides many food and drink tents, there are other activities which include dancing, a baby show, a fashion show, local live entertainment, a

magic act and a demonstration by police dogs. There is also a show by the Cayman Islands Equestrian Federation which includes lead line and cross rail jumping, a Parelli demonstration, gymkhana games and a costume competition for horses and riders.

▲ Calf

▲ Horses carry flags at the opening ceremony of the Agricultural Show

▲ Governor Jack opening the Agricultural Show 2007

▲ Produce in Show

'Rundown' – February/March

'Rundown' is a showcase for satirical comedy from the Cayman Islands with colourful costumes, great sets and a very talented cast. The seventeenth rundown (2008) was written by Dave Martins, directed by Henry Muttoo and jointly produced by the Cayman National Cultural Foundation and Dave Martins. For further information and tickets, contact CNCF, tel 949 5477, eayfest@candw.ky, www.artscayman.org.

Cayman Classic – March

This food and wine festival showcases the best of the island's traditional dishes and international cuisine. It consists of four days of cooking demonstrations by both overseas celebrity chefs and native, island chefs. A popular gala dinner and wine-tasting events are features of the festival. It attracts many 'foodies' from all over the world. For information, contact the Department of Tourism, tel 949 0623 or www.caymanislands.ky.

Cayfest – April

This is the Cayman Islands' National Festival of the Arts and is a major production organised by the Cayman National Cultural Foundation with events on all three islands including performing, culinary, literary and visual arts. For information contact the CNCF, tel 949 5477, cayfest@candw.ky or www.artscayman.org.

Batabano – May

Batabano is Cayman's annual carnival when soca and calypso bands play while people parade in fantastic costumes. Floats from districts all over the Islands compete for the 'best adorned truck' and other awards. There is also a junior carnival, street dance and masquerade fête at Pedro St James. For information, contact www.caymancarnival. com.

International Fishing Tournament – February to May

The Cayman Islands' Angling Club organises a number of tournaments every year from February to May including the annual spring International Tournament with prize money of about $400,000.

Pirates Week – November

This is the main festival in Cayman's calendar. It reflects the Islands' seafaring past and everyone becomes a pirate – it is possible to see Blackbeard, Captain Henry Morgan and Anne Bonny all walking the streets of George Town. Some people even go to work as a pirate. There is a fun run, the Miss Festival Queen competition, street dancing, a food festival and fireworks. Pirates come ashore at Hog Sty Bay in George Town to take the Governor hostage and put him in the stocks. Floats parade through the town and all districts and companies take part in the competitions. Each district celebrates Heritage Day which has been amalgamated into Pirate Week and traditional crafts, arts and music are exhibited. At the end of the week, the wicked pirates are put on trial so that life can return to normal. For information contact www.piratesweekfestival.com or tel 949 5859.

▲ Pirate and daughter

Gimistory – November

During this international storytelling festival people gather to hear enchanting and jovial stories and duppy tales which are told accompanied by music, mime and dance all around the islands at historic and picturesque locations such as Smith Cove, the courtyard at Camana Bay and Pedro Castle. Local dishes of fried fish and fritters and swankie (lemonade) are served. For information contact the Cayman National Cultural Foundation www.artscayman.org.

Jazz Fest – December

In 2008 the fifth Jazz Festival took place. Previous performers have included Natalie Cole, Al Jarreau and various local bands. It is organised by the Department of Tourism. For information, contact www.caymanislands.ky/jazzfest.

Al Jarreau ▶

Christmas – December

There is a Christmas House Lighting Contest which encourages Cayman to look just like the opening scenes in the film *The Grinch who Stole Christmas* starring Jim Carrey! There are lights everywhere, even on palm trees and boats. Carols are sung on the steps of George Town's Courthouse and there are tree lighting ceremonies and a special Santa Claus landing.

Entertainment

Cayman Islands National Dance Company – Dance Unlimited, founded in 1988 by Lorna Reid, performs at the Prospect Playhouse and the Harquail Theatre, tel 947 6616.

Cayman National Choir, tel 949 7800.

Harquail Theatre, West Bay Road – stages five major productions a year tel 949 5054.

Prospect Playhouse, Red Bay, tel 949 5477 – a 330-seat community theatre.

Marquee Cinema – shows several movies every day, tel 949 2632. Adults: CI$10, children CI$6.50.

Dart Cinema, Camana Bay

The Hollywood Theatres – the six-screen cinema at Camana Bay. Check www.gohollywood.com for film times

All Fired Up, tel 947 8517 – here you can decorate a pottery item and paint it with glaze. It takes up to two weeks to fire so make sure you allow time. If you are not here that long then you can work on a mosaic. Open six days a week from 10.00–18.00.

Spas

Silver Rain at the Ritz Carlton – is the only La Prairie spa in the Caribbean. It is well worth booking a treatment here as the interior is gorgeous. It is all slate, silver and white leather with lots of white lilies. The changing rooms are beautiful, complete with steam rooms and jacuzzis.

▲ Silver Rain

Hibiscus Spa at the Westin Casuarina, tel 945 3800, is right next to the Westin on Seven Mile Beach and has excellent treatments in a luxurious interior.

Tips 'N Toes, Bayshore Mall, Harbour Driver/ Goring Avenue, George Town, tel 943 8638 – go here for the fabulous manicures, nail extensions and pedicures.

◄ The Girls at Tips 'N Toes

▲ Harbour Drive

SHOPPING

Along **Harbour Drive, Cardinall Avenue** and the other main streets of George Town very near to the cruise ship terminal, you can find many shops selling world-renowned luxury brands such as Cartier, Waterford, Wedgwood, Fossil, Swatch, Colombian Emeralds, Bernard K Passman, Rolex, Omega, Breitling, Tag Heuer, David Yurman, Fendi, Gucci, Longchamp, Guerlain, Chopard, Bulgari, Lalique, Calvin Klein and Ralph Lauren also perfume and cosmetics. This area is very safe and very clean. Harley Davidson and Hard Rock Café are also here and George Town is a Disney World style of town.

For **lingerie and beachwear shops**, Natalie Bishop at Harbour Place, South Church Street and the Beachwear Shop at Treasure Island Resort both stock clothing by very exclusive designers. The Ritz Carlton has Wave and the very chic shop just outside the Silver Rain Spa which sells beachwear and jewellery.

Natalie Bishop ▶

The **Book Nook**, Galleria Plaza on West Bay Road stocks absolutely any book you could possibly want. The shop is brilliant and also sells a large variety of toys and art materials. Other book shops are **Hobbies and Books** opposite the police station on Elgin Avenue, George Town and **Books & Books**, 45 Market Street, Camana Bay stocking current English, American and local books.

▲ George Town branch of the Book Nook with children from East End Primary School

For **Tortuga Rum Cake**, made from a secret 100 year-old family recipe, visit the shop founded in 1984 by husband and wife team Robert and Carlene Hamaty. There are seven different flavours available. Contact www.tortugarums.com for worldwide delivery.

Visit **Guy Harvey** for wine from California.

Absolutely Fabulous, at the Caymanian Village, tel 916 3312, is a wonderful interior design shop which sells furniture, frames, vases, bowls and artwork – all imported from Indonesia.

Absolutely Fabulous ▶

Look out also for **Hell Sauce, Cayman Soap, Cayman Sea Salt, Hawley Haven Preserves, Cayman Tropicals,** and **Dready** products created by Shane Aquart. The **Bakery** on Mary Street opposite the Lobster Pot on North Church Street sells delicious treats and coffee and tea.

Mr Arthur's Grocery Store on North Church Street, which was registered as a grocery store in 1897 but has actually been here much longer, is run by Arthurlyn Bodden. The beautiful traditional Caymanian house and print shop across the road belonged to her father Arthur Bodden.

▲ Arthurlyn Bodden

▲ Mr Arthur's Grocery Store

Fresh fish is sold daily in the **fish market** on George Town Harbour, in the area called Hog Sty Bay and you can choose what you want from parrotfish, jack, grunt, yellowtail barracuda, mahi mahi, mackerel, butterfish or grouper. The fishermen will clean, fillet and wash the fish and even give advice about cooking it!

Fish market ▶

Dr Carey's Black Coral Clinic on South Church Street – you can't miss this as there is a yellow sign near the roadside clearly marking it. You go into a driveway and can park outside the hut that is Dr Carey's Black Coral Clinic, called the 'Bikini Hut' because of his large collection of bikinis – donations welcome. Dr Carey, who was a merchant seaman in his time, also has a large collection of marbles and, alongside his carved black coral pieces, sells shells too. This hut is right on the beach.

◀ Dr Carey's Bikini Hut

Cathy Church's Photographic Centre and Gallery is on South Church Street and sells digital cameras for above and underwater photography. Here you can also sign up for an underwater photography course. Cathy has been on the island since 1972.

Fresh Caymanian produce is sold at the **fruit and vegetable market** held in the Agricultural Pavilion, Savannah on Saturdays. All sorts of fruit and vegetables are available including pineapples, mangos, bananas, soursops, oranges, grapefruit, limes and lemons, cassava breadfruit, cabbages, plantains, yams, ackee and peppers – all produced on local farms such as Red Mole (named after the red earth in the area) and Whistling Duck in North Side.

The **Cayman craft market** is located on the junction of South Church Street and Boilers Road and overlooks George Town Harbour. Here you can buy jams and jellies from the Whistling Duck Farm in North Side, saltwater taffy from the Cayman taffy company, pickled peppers and pepper sauces, island fudge, Cayman sea salt, black coral and caymanite jewellery, thatch work hats and bags, and waurie boards for playing the local version of the international game played with cayman 'knickers' (a type of seed) or marbles. It is open from Monday to Friday, 08.30–15.00.

The **Grand Harbour Shopping Centre** is located just off the roundabout at the junction of South Sound Road. Here is the Black Pearl Skate and Surf Park and the restaurant the Black Pearl Galley. There is Hobbies and Books, a video and games shop, a craft shop and a huge supermarket. It is beautifully designed in traditional Cayman style. Don't miss Willie's jams and jellies roadside stall, about 200 yards east of Hurley's, which mostly sells fruit and vegetables.

▲ Aerial view of Grand Harbour Shopping Centre and Black Pearl Skate and Surf Park

Activities

Golf

Two of the main tournaments are the Cayman Islands Chamber of Commerce Golf Classic and the Cinco de Mayo Corona Golf Tournament at the Links. Golf is a major activity on Grand Cayman. For information, contact Britannia Golf Club, tel 949 1234.

Sailing

There are many companies on the Island that charter boats but try **Red Baron Charters** tel 916 4333 or 945 4744. Neil Galway, a RYA Yacht Master, offers sailing swimming and snorkelling adventures. He runs two boats the *Red Baron* (39 ft) and the *Nautigal* (44 ft) for luxury cruising excursions for any amount of time you wish.

The **Cayman Catboat Association**, tel 925 7217. The Cayman catboat is the traditional turtling vessel used throughout the Islands' history. They are small boats which were loaded onto schooners for the long journeys to catch turtles. A catboat is always displayed at Cayfest, the Caymanian Festival of the Arts.

Xanax Sailing Cruises, tel 949 1186 – take a cruise aboard the 32 foot *Erickson*. Dinner cruises are also available.

Supersail Cayman Maxi Challenge, tel 925 6294, offer two three-hour sailings per day. You can take part in the race or sit back, relax and watch. After a 45 minute warm up, the Maxi Match Race begins along Seven Mile Beach. There is a prize giving after the regatta at Sunset House on South Church Street.

Thriller Adventure Tour, tel 324 0520 – offshore yellow and red racing boats take you along the shoreline of Grand Cayman to the Turtle Farm and Seven Mile Beach.

The **Governor's Cup** is held in mid-July and attracts many racing teams from all over the world.

Hiking

The best hiking can be found on the **Mastic Trail** which is on the Mastic Reserve. The National Trust organises guided hikes. These are two-mile adventures which take about three hours and are led by a naturalist. You enter Cayman's interior and hear the song of the many indigenous birds, see the original dry forest, bat caves and many other hidden treasures. The Trust organises lunch in Old Man Bay, Breakers or East End. Mangrove boat cruises take place in the evening, when it is cooler, and take the short trip across North Sound to the central mangroves. The National Trust also organises snorkelling trips, nature walks, historic walking tours, native craft demonstrations, local heritage presentations and bird-watching. For information, contact the National Trust, tel 949 0121 or www.nationaltrust.org.ky

Horse riding

Horse riding is a wonderful experience in Cayman, either along the beach or on interior trails throughout the Island. You can book early morning rides or choose to ride at sunset to avoid the main heat of the day. Call the **Equestrian Federation**, tel 516 1751, for a list of stables or try **Coral Stone Stables**, tel 916 4799 or www.csstables.com. These stables have 25 horses on 10 acres of land. On your ride along the beaches you will see frigate birds, whistling ducks, herons and the local flora and fauna.

Pampered Ponies, tel 945 2262, offer private rides and group rides in the early morning and sunset rides along the beach.

Kayaking

Kayak Safaris, tel 949 7700, are run by the same company as Atlantis Submarines. This involves kayaking around the wetlands which is very good exercise. The two-hour guided safari begins in South Sound, tours the red mangroves and you may snorkel with fish, conch and lobster.

▲ South Sound kayaking

Cayman Kayaks, tel 926 4467 offer tandem and single kayaks and explore the central wetlands. They depart from Kaibo Beach Bar and Grill.

Surfing

Cayman is not a prime surfing destination as the waves are very inconsistent, but when the conditions are right, great surfing is to be had on South Sound Beach, at East End and Bodden Town. You have to wear reef boots as the waves break on very sharp rocks, which are sometimes covered with sea urchins.

Kite-surfing – the best place for kite-surfing is Barker's Beach in West Bay where you can learn with an instructor.

▲ Dayne Brummet and Josh Palmer-Ebanks at Black Pearl

Black Pearl Skate and Surf Park, tel 947 4161 – opened by the world's most famous skater Tony Hawk, Black Pearl is the second largest outdoor concrete skate park with 62 000 square feet of bowls and half pipes. You can rent the boards, helmets and elbow, knee and wrist pads. You can buy either an unlimited day session pass or a tourist one-week pass. There are occasionally courses run with professional skaters from the US. The surf park produces artificial waves up to 11 feet high. There is an annual membership available if you are resident. The park runs weekly shows.

◄ Skate lesson

Fitness Connexion, tel 949 8485 – here is the Be Active Centre which offers swimming, snorkelling, scuba diving, karate, dance, soccer at the adventure club and holiday camps. Visiting children can join in all programmes.

Kings Sports Centre, tel 946 5464 – offers 35 000 square feet of action, including a powerhouse gym, steam rooms and studio rooms for aerobic and martial arts classes. There is also an indoor cycling arena, squash courts, a rock climbing wall, a party room, a video arcade and an indoor sports rink for football, basketball, hockey and roller skating.

Cayman Helicopters, tel 525 6967 or www.caymanislandshelicopters.com, offer various tours – the Seven Mile Beach Tour which is 10 minutes long; the Stingray Tour which flies around the horseshoe bay of North Sound and over the crystalline waters of the sandbar where you can see the stingrays from above; or a whole island tour which takes 45 minutes to fly over all the main attractions of Grand Cayman – Pedro Castle, the Lighthouse at Breakers, the Wreck of the Ten Sails at East End, Rum Point, North Sound, Seven Mile Beach and George Town Harbour. Book online for a discount. Cayman Helicopters can tailor your trip to suit your needs and can even transport you to dinner, landing at either the Ritz Carlton or Pappagallo's.

▲ Cayman Helicopters

Grand Cayman Hog Riders, tel 943 8699 or www.hogriders.com – you can ride a hog, otherwise known as a Harley Davidson, by booking at the office at 161 North Church Street. The Harley Davidson shop is further down the road, opposite the harbour.

Cayman Hog Riders ▶

The **Rugby Club**, tel 949 7960 is in South Sound – call if you want to catch one of the games.

SUBMARINES

Atlantis, tel 949 7700 or www.atlantisadventures.com – this is how you can see underwater life without learning to dive! The hour-long tour goes close to the reefs where a wide variety of fish and sea creatures can be seen. The clarity of the water is amazing and the submarine goes to a depth of 30 metres (100 feet). You can see angelfish, snappers, barrel sponges, star corals, sea turtles, stingrays, barracuda, groupers and moray eels. The submarine hovers over the Cayman Wall which plunges to at least 600 metres (1500 feet). There is a spectacular view over the breathtaking drop. The *Seaworld Explorer*, which is a semi-submarine, is also available for viewing shallow reefs.

Bubble sub, tel 943 3283 – again, if you don't snorkel or dive this is the best way of seeing under the water. The bubble sub goes to a depth of 120 metres (40 feet) and carries two passengers in a watertight glass bubble giving you a 360° view. A diver drives the submarine and feeds the fish, attracting shoals of bar jacks. You can communicate with your diver throughout the trip, so you can direct your own trip.

▲ The Nautilus semi-submarine docked by Hammerheads pub on the waterfront, George Town

Nautilus Undersea Tours, tel 945 1355 – these are semi-submarines and from them you can view the shipwrecks of the *Cali* and the *Balboa*. You also stop at Cheeseburger Reef (near Burger King) where a diver feeds the fish. There are two trips, one of an hour and another of an hour and a half which also includes snorkelling at Cheeseburger Reef.

Cayman Deep See Experience, tel 926 3343 or www.deepseecayman.com – this is an amazing experience allowing you to see what lives in the sea deeper than the height of two Empire State Buildings. These are depths unreachable by scuba diving or technical diving. The camera-equipped robot, *Little Tyche*, transmits real time video footage of the abundant, strange phenomena found in the total darkness of the sea's mesopelagic

▲ Portrait of Gary Montemayor

'twilight' zone. Guided by an award winning videographer, rarely seen creatures are viewed by you on HDTV screens in the control room of the luxury yacht *Deep Seeker*. This is a unique adventure that can be included in your vacation itinerary. You can pilot the underwater robot (ROV) or tell the pilot where you want to go. **Gary Montemayor** is the videographer in charge and he has an impressive pedigree. From 1991 to 1996 he was a submersible pilot in Maui and Honolulu in Hawaii and also participated in the building of the largest submersible in the world, which took place in Everett, Washington. From 1996 to 2004, Gary worked for the Research Submersibles in the Cayman Islands, completing a few thousand dives into the mesopelagic zone 240–360 metres (800–1200 feet) down. He was the main pilot and deep sea guide for the filming of the *Blue Planet* in the Cayman Islands. During this shoot, they came across the largest shark ever filmed. Gary, more recently, was the test pilot for the world's most expensive private submarine and the chief pilot for all underwater vehicles for the largest yacht in the world, *The Octopus*, which included an ROV, a submarine and a hyperbaric chamber. The expedition takes two hours and group rates are available.

Jolly Roger and Anne Bonny Cruises, tel 945 7245 – these run two-hour cruises which create pirate adventures for children on recreated seventeenth-century pirate boats. The crew are dressed as

pirates and put the children to work swabbing the deck and shooting cannons at passing ships. Two unlucky parents are tied up and subjected to iced water torture. The boats tour

◀ Jumping off the *Anne Bonny*

Seven Mile Beach and anchor for an hour so that you may jump off the high sides of the boat and walk the plank. The *Jolly Roger* and *Anne Bonny* also run dinner cruises. There is another boat, the *Penzance* which is a 1960's, Bond-style yacht which can be hired for charters along with gourmet meals.

Snorkelling

There are many snorkelling sites on Grand Cayman. Anywhere on Seven Mile Beach is worth trying, also at the sandbar and Stingray City when you are on a tour. Healthy snacks for fish – which will attract them – are frozen peas and squid. **Red Sail Sports** can take you out on one of their catamarans to snorkel or to go to Stingray City. Here is a selection of other popular snorkelling sites.

Eden Rock – near to Paradise Bar and Grill where you will see sargeant majors, bermuda chubs, yellowtail snappers, parrotfish, tarpon, stingrays and sea turtles.

Wreck of the Cali – 50 yards out near Rackham's or Hammerhead's pubs on the waterfront in George Town, where an old sailing ship used as a freighter rests in 60 metres (20 feet) of water. The ship was carrying dry grain and rice which swelled up when it took on water and sank the ship.

Cheeseburger Reef – also known as Soto's reef after the famed diver Bob Soto. It is called Cheeseburger Reef because it is straight out from Burger King. Here you can see tarpon, sea turtles, tunnels and swim-throughs and the coral is very colourful.

Cemetery Reef – 50 yards out from the beach on the West Bay Road, where you can see blue tangs, parrotfish, yellowtail snappers, blue striped grunts, blue-headed wrasses, four eyed butterfly fish, bar jacks and black durgeon.

Coral Gardens – accessible by boat and part of the barrier reef near the sandbar. Here there are moray eels, queen conch shells and all sorts of coral.

▲ *Spirit of Cayman*, Red Sail Sports' catamaran on Seven Mile Beach

SPORT FISHING

The Cayman Islands' Angling Club organises a number of tournaments every year from February to May, including the annual spring International Tournament with prize money of about $400000.

Varieties of fish that can be caught include:

Yellowfin tuna (*Thunnus albacares*) which are great to watch as they jump high out of the water and are strong fighters on the line. The best bait is cut up fish and squid.

Blue Marlin (*Makaira nigricans*) which grow to well over 1000 lbs in weight (average size 200lbs) and which also make amazing leaps from the water.

Wahoo (*Acanthocybium solandri*) which are the fastest fish and can move at about 45 mph. They are caught during the cooler months from November onwards. Ballyhoo is good bait for Wahoo.

Mahi mahi (*Coryphaena hyppurus*) which are also known as dolphin – but bearing no relation to 'Flipper' the dolphin – and dorado, and which chase schools of flying fish which again is great to see.

Grouper and **Snapper** are everywhere and are very easy to catch.

Tarpon (*Magalops atlanticus*) which can grow to well over 200 lbs, are the largest member of the herring family. They are full of bones and no good to eat, so definitely a 'catch-and-release' fish.

Bone fish (*Albula vulpes*) which is found in shallow waters and is hard to catch as it is very smart.

In the flats at North Sound, you can catch small crabs that live in the turtle grass.

There are many knowledgeable local captains that have been navigating the waters around the Island for years that can take you out to fish:

Crosby's Watersports, tel 916 1725 – Crosby is one of the original captains. As the Barefoot Man has described Captain Crosby, he 'can navigate the North Sound blindfolded, and after a day of snorkelling, fishing and making conch salad you can find him at the Royal Palms teaching some sunburned visitor how to dance a calypso'.

▲ Captain Crosby Ebanks

Captain Marvin's Watersports, tel 945 4590, **Bayside Watersports**, tel 949 3200, **R & M Fly Shop and Charters** (Captain Ronald Ebanks is one of the most experienced fly fishermen), **Oh Boy Charters**, tel 949 6341, **Clinton's Watersports**, tel 949 3054, **Black Princess Charters**, tel 949 0400, **Frank's Watersports**, tel 945 5491, are all members of the Cayman National Watersports Association, www.captainmarvins.com.

Stingray City

You can choose from two areas from which to view the stingrays in Grand Cayman. There is a 12 foot area in North Sound where you can snorkel, swim and dive, or there is the sandbar near the barrier reef where the water is waist deep, crystal clear and turquoise, so you can stand or even kneel with the stingrays. The sandbar is ideal if you are not a diver as you don't need fins or a snorkel. However, you do need to shuffle your feet along the sand in a walk called the 'stingray shuffle' to avoid lifting your feet and taking large steps when you might inadvertently stand on a stingray. You can feed the stingrays in both areas with squid. Captain Marvin Ebanks, who is 90 years old, is one of the first locals to have brought tourists to the area. In the past, fishermen couldn't clean the fish on shore because of the mosquitoes, so they used to clean fish on the sandbar and the stingrays came for the scraps. This is how the area was discovered as an excellent place to take the tourists. Caymanian captains first began taking tourists to the spot in 1951 and they know the area well. This community of rays is friendly. The males are much smaller and more timid than the females. (The darker the skin the older they are.) They have rough-textured upper backs, similar to shark-skin, and their underside is velvety smooth. Divers say each stingray has a distinct personality, just like a dog or a cat.

Don Fosters of the Sun Rayz team ▶ holding a stingray

The main defence mechanism of stingrays is to bury themselves in the sand. They hunt by using a very keen sense of smell and use electroreceptors on the underside of their body, to detect minute electrical currents and vibrations in order to find food. Their favourite food are crustaceans and molluscs. Stingrays are ovoviparous which means their offspring are gestated within eggs rather than in a placenta. The eggs hatch inside the mother's body

before the young are born and the gestation period is four months. Three to five babies are born at any one time and the baby stingrays are four to six inches across their wingspan. They are left to fend for themselves as they are abandoned by their mother as soon as they are born.

▲ A stingray

DIVING

Diving is perfect in the Cayman Islands – the water is warm, buoyant and very, very clear. Beautiful, unspoilt reefs line the shores of all three islands and the undersea gardens are breathtaking with many corals and fish in the clear waters. There are countless wrecks which have accumulated over the centuries and each has its own story to tell.

There are many excellent instructors that make you feel comfortable and safe – if you have any worries, a visit to Cathy Church at her Sunset House in South Church Street will calm you initial nerves before learning to dive. She will assure you that the adventure is worth it and even teach you to photograph underwater before your trip is over.

▲ Cathy Church's underwater photography class at Sunset House

▲ Coming back from a dive just outside Cracked Conch, West Bay

Philippe Cousteau and David Doubilet, famous National Geographic photographers, are fans of the diving on Cayman. On Grand Cayman, the wall on the North Shore is lined with pinnacles topped by rare black corals. Here you can see sharks, rays and turtles as well as a wide variety of tropical fish. The Wall is a sheer underwater drop-off which starts at a depth of 60 metres (20 feet). Cayman Brac has walls on both sides – the southern wall has sheer drop-offs and vertical swim-throughs, tunnels and grottos.

Dive hotels

Brac Reef Resort, brac@reefseas.com – Brac has the wreck of the soviet warship the MV *Captain Keith Tibetts* and also the Lost City of Atlantis – underwater concrete statues sculpted by Caymanian artist Foots and which are already showing new coral growth. The sculptures cause no impact or destruction of existing coral or marine life as they are all placed on sand.

Little Cayman Beach Resort, bestdiving@reefseas.com

Compass Point Dive Resort, tel 345 947 7500 or www.compasspoint.ky – staff can arrange dives on all of the East End reefs as well as the wall dives. The resort has excellent facilities and its own dive boats and dock. There are 18 one and two-bedroom suites.

The Agressor IV, tel 949 5551 or www.aggressor.com – is a 'live aboard' dive boat and has luxurious ensuite cabins.

Don Foster's Dive, Cayman, Casuarina Point, South Church Street, tel 943 5679

Don Foster's on South Church Street ▶

Dive Tech, tel 345 946 5658 or www.divetech.com – offer diving holidays at Turtle Reef or Cobalt Coast.

Quabo Dive, tel 945 4769 – is run by Arthle Evans, one of the first Caymanian dive instructors.

Red Sail Sports
Hyatt Regency, tel 949 8745
Marriott Resort, tel 949 6343
Rum Point, tel 947 0203
Westin Resort, tel 949 8723
Marriott Courtyard, tel 946 4433

At Red Sail Sports, Hyatt ▶

Eden Rock Diving Centre, South Church Street, tel 949 7243

Sunset House, South Church Street, tel 949 7111

Ocean Frontiers, tel 947 7500

Divers Down Seven Mile Beach, tel 916 3751

Wall to Wall Diving, tel 945 6608

GETTING DIVE CERTIFIED

You can dive without being certified by just filling out a waiver and a questionnaire about your physical health. All dives are made under the supervision of a master level dive instructor and do not go below 105 metres (35 feet).

You still have to go into a classroom with an instructor where you learn about the equipment, the effects of increased water pressure and how to use hand signals to communicate with other divers. You then go into a swimming pool for a couple of hours' practice where you get to use weights and an inflatable vest called a BCD and the breathing apparatus – an oxygen tank and a regulator. Here you practice breathing under water, how to clear your scuba mask if water gets in it and how to equalise the pressure in your ears (more intense than on a plane flight).

If you want to learn to dive without an instructor you have to sign up for the full **Professional Association of Diving Instructors (PADI)** open water diver's course.

The PADI open water diver's manual is about 250 pages long with five chapters. Each chapter has a test at the end. Your answers will be checked by an instructor. You then take a 50 question test – you will need to get at least 75 per cent right.

▲ Dive boat

After passing the test, you need to swim at least 200 metres and tread or float in water for 10 minutes.

You practice removing and replacing your scuba mask while underwater, breathing from a dive companion's air supply, towing an injured or panicked diver to safety and how to deal with equipment malfunction.

The final exam requires that you have completed at least four separate underwater dives before getting PADI certification. You must record the time and depth of each dive on a chart that you are given.

▼ Diving in George Town

The pressure increases the deeper you go and your air runs out faster. The Cayman Islands is considered the best snorkelling and diving in the Caribbean. The visibility is excellent – the water is very clear. The conservation policies are strict, so this encourages a good marine life and ensures that the reefs and walls are protected as much as possible. Most diving is supervised by the **Cayman Islands Tourism Association** (CITA). They train all the dive masters and instructors. The CITA is a fully membership-funded, private sector organisation representing over 220 businesses from all sectors of the tourism industry in Cayman. It represents over 50 watersports and dive operators and maintains marine conservation, education, safety standards and high quality instruction.

It is possible to do three dives in the course of 24 hours – a shallow dive to 18m (60ft), a deep dive to 30m (100ft) and then a night dive. On the 100-foot dives, the CITA recommends a safety stop on the way to the surface – about 3–5 minutes at 10 feet.

Underwater protocol
The Department of Environment has a list of matters to be aware of while diving or snorkelling. For more information on marine conservation, contact them on tel 949 8469, or the Cayman Islands Tourism Association, PO Box 31086 SMB, Grand Cayman, tel 949 8522 or www.cita.ky.

Buoyancy control
You have to be properly weighted in order to control yourself on the reef. If over weighted, you are more likely to crash into and damage the reef.

Move gracefully underwater. Experienced divers are relatively still. Movement is calm and fluid and hands are hardly ever used for movement. If you accidentally touch the reef, stop and breathe in. This will lift you off the reef without any movement on your part.

Watch your console and octopus. If you are trailing either, they can scrape and break the coral.

Gloves are prohibited – if your hands are bare, you will take much greater care about what you put them on. You might be damaging microscopic coral larvae colonising what, in 100 years' time will be a beautiful piece of coral.

Watch your fins and be careful not to break the coral and kick up sand and sediment which will smother the coral.

Try to limit fish feeding as it distorts the fish populations leading to an unstable ecological balance or create a pool of fish dependent of handouts.

While photographing fish, move carefully towards your subject and stay buoyant rather than resting on coral. When you have finished, move away carefully.

Most of the sites have a mooring buoy to avoid coral damages. If there is no buoy, the operators make sure they let their anchor down onto a sandy area. Most dive boats are flat-bed boats with twin outboard motors. They have a shallow draft and can come directly onto the beach to load passengers and air cylinders. The journeys to dive sites normally take about 15–20 minutes. Travelling to the North Wall from Seven Mile Beach and West Bay takes about 35–45 minutes.

Cayman fish

Stingrays (*Dasyatis americana*). Found at Stingray City and the sandbar on Grand Cayman, they are easily approached and friendly and you can feed them squid, but be careful of the stinger on the tail! There are other species of ray to be found in the Caymans: Manta Ray (*Manta birostris*) can be seen along the Bloody Bay wall in Little Cayman. The Spotted Eagle Ray (*Aetobatus narinari*) is also large and has a pig's snout which it uses to forage for crustaceans and molluscs. The Electric, or Torpedo Ray (*Torpedo nobiliana*) is smaller and grows to a length of 1.5 metres (5 feet). This ray has two organs to stun prey with an electrical charge of between 14 and 37 volts. The Yellow Stingray (*Urolophus jamaicenseis*) grows to 50 centimetres (15 inches) and is circular with a strong tail and a poisonous spine

Groupers. There are up to 16 different types, including the Nassau Grouper (*Epinephelus striatus*). The largest grouper is the Jawfish (*Epinephelus itajara*) which can grow to 2 metres (5 feet) long. There is also the Coney (*Cephalopholis fulvus*) which is smaller and grows to 40 centimetres (16 inches).

Creole fish (*Paranthias furcifer*) live in the large vase sponges. The Fairy Basslet (*Gramma loreto*) is very small at 7.5 centimetres (3 inches) and is brightly coloured purple and violet with a yellow tail.

Snappers. Various species of snapper may be seen, including the Yellowtail Snapper (*Ocyurus chrysurus*) which are found in large schools, the Schoolmaster (*Lutjanus apodus*) and the Bluestriped Grunt (*haemulon sciurus*).

White margates (*Haemulon album*) are a pearl, grey-blue colour and are commonly seen with the White Grunt (*Haemulon plumieri*) which has blue stripes on its head.

Parrotfish. Princess Parrotfish (*Scarus taeniopterus*) grow to 10–18 centimetres (4–7 inches) and the male grows to 32 centimetres (13 inches).

A larger parrotfish is the Spotlight Parrotfish (*Sparisoma viride*). The male of this species can grow to 60 centimetres (2 feet). These fish are the most beautiful colours: turquoise, orange, yellow, blue and purple.

Hogfish (*Lachnolaimus maximus*) grow to 1 metre (3 feet) in length and are found near feeding stingrays. The Spanish Hogfish (*Bodianus rufus*) are smaller, but much more brightly-coloured with a purple upper body and golden yellow belly and tail.

Blenny. Peppermint Goby (*Coryphopterus lipernes*) swim in short bursts of speed because the do not have swim bladders. The Cleaning Goby (*Gobiosoma genie*) may also be found.

Squirrelfish (*Holocentrus adscensionis*) is red in colour with horizontal silvery stripes and has triangular, white markings on the tips of its dorsal spines. The Bigeye (*Priacanthus arenatus*) does not have these markings but is all red.

Bar jack (*Carnax ruber*) mates are different colours – one stays silver blue and the other turns black and looks, and acts, like the other's shadow. They are often seen feeding with the stingrays. They swim in large schools. Other silver fish, which are also seen in large schools, are the Saucer Eye Porgy (*Calamus calamus*) and the Bermuda Chub (*Kyphosus sectatrix*).

Silversides, including the herring, anchovy and scad species. These are small silver fish that grow to 8 centimetres (3 inches) long. These are a wonderful sight when seen in large schools.

Wrasse. There are several species to be found, the largest of which grows to 50 centimetres (18 inches). This is the Pudding Wife (*Halichoeres radiatus*) which is a blue-green fish with markings on its head. Other species are the Bluehead Wrasse (*Thalassoma bifasciatum*) and the Yellowhead Wrasse (*Halichoeres garnoti*).

Butterflyfish. There are six species of butterfly fish, the most stunning being the Foureye Butterflyfish (*Chaetodon capistratus*) – with its black and white stripes which blend to gold on the outside on its wide, flat body and a distinctive black spot surrounded with white which looks like an eye near the tail – and the Spotfin Butterfly fish (*Chaetodon ocellatus*) which has a white body with a yellow trim and a black vertical band through the face and eye.

Angelfish (*Holacanthus ciliariaris*) grow to 45 centimetres (18 inches) and are an amazing colour. They have an electric-blue body, gold fins, tail and face and a noticeable crown on the head.

Trumpetfish (*Aulostomus maculates*) can grow to 1.8 metres (5 feet) long and are many colours from red to yellow. The fish gets its name from its trumpet-shaped mouth. The Cornetfish grows to the same size and has blue spots on its body.

Scorpion fish. These are more visible at night and have amazing camouflage abilities. Be careful as they sting!

Damselfish includes the Sergeant Major (*Abudefduf saxatilis*), a yellow and black striped fish which grows to 17 centimetres (7 inches) and the Yellowtail Damselfish (*Microspathodon chtysurus*) which is smaller and has a dark body with iridescent blue spots on its back and a yellow tail.

Eels. The Green Moray (*Gymnothorax funebris*) is the largest of the eels in the Caymans. They can grow up to 1.8 metres (5 feet) long. The Spotted Moray (*Gymnothorax*) can grow up to 60 centimetres (2 feet) long and is the most common. The Goldentail Moray (*Gymnothorax miliaris*) is brown with yellow spots and is even smaller. You are lucky if you see a Chain Moray (*Echidna catenata*) which has a dark brown or black body with yellow bars and eyes, or a Garden Eel (*Heteroconger halis*) which is very shy.

Tarpon (*Megalops atlanticus*) can grow up to 2.4 metres (10 feet) and are silvery in colour.

Tarpon ▶

Pufferfish. These and the porcupine and ballon fish and should not be touched as they can become easily diseased.

Sharks. These are not very common, although if you are lucky, you might see a Nurse Shark (*Ginglymostoma cirratum*).

Invertebrates

Jellyfish and hydroids. These are very closely related, the only difference being that the jellyfish is free swimming. Anemones are also related and can sting. In the Caymans, you can see the Giant Anemone (*Condylactis gigantean*) and the Corkscrew Anemone (*Bartholomea annulata*). The Moon Jellyfish (*Aurelia aurita*) is very common as is the Portuguese Man-of-War with its long tentacles which can grow to 10 metres (35 feet) long.

Worms. The colourful, social Feather Duster Worm (*Bispira brunnea*), the Magnificent Feather Duster Worm *sabellastartia magnifica* and the Christmas Tree Worm (*Spirobranchus giganteus*) at 3 centimetres (2.5 inches) high come in a wide variety of colours.

Bearded Fire Worm (*Hermodice carunculata*) grows to 15 centimetres (6 inches) long. The fine hairs on its body can irritate the skin.

Sponges are very delicate and you must be very careful not to touch them. Yellow Tube Sponge (*Aplysina fistularis*), Pink Vase Sponge (*Niphates digitalis*) and Rope Sponges *Aaplysina cauliformis* and *Aplysina fulva* may be found. The most stunning of the sponges is the Giant Barrel Sponge (*Xestospongia muta*).

Shrimps. Amongst the shrimps that may be found are the Peppermint Shrimp (*Lysmata wurdemanni*), the red Night Shrimp (*Rhynchocinetes rigens*), which has bright green eyes at night, and the Coral Banded Shrimp (*Stenopus hispidus*) which is small with long pincers.

Lobsters and hermit crabs. Spiny Lobster (*Panulirus argus*), the White Speckled Hermit Crab (*Paguristed punticeps*) which can grow up to 12 centimetres (5 inches) and the Red Reef Hermit Crab (*Paguristes cadenati*) may all be found.

Molluscs. The Queen Conch (*Strombus gigas*) is caught for eating. The Atlantic Deer Cowrie (*Cyprae cervus*) and the Flamingo Tongue (*Cyphoma gibbosum*) which has a speckled shell may also be found.

Nudibranchs these are very brightly coloured. Also, look out for octopus and squid, starfish, sea urchins and sea cucumbers.

Dive flags have to be used when diving is in progress. The flag is rectangular and red with a diagonal white stripe.

Both one and two-tank dives are available and a charge will be made to cover the cost of hiring weights and a tank of air. You do not need suits, hoods or gloves because of the temperature of the water. You may gain the PADI Open Water Certification, or, through Discover Scuba courses, take a PADI refresher course if it is a few years since your last dive. Snorkelling equipment is also available for hire.

Decompression chamber

The hyperbaric chamber is run by the Cayman Islands' Government (contact tel 949 2989 or 555 for any diving-related emergency). There have been 600 treatments since the chamber opened in 1972. Incidents can happen because of a build up of nitrogen over a one or two week stay when diving three or more dives per day. All divers know that they must take time to surface from a dive to avoid the bends or decompression sickness.

Dive sites

These are numerous – there are about 1000 dive sites recorded on all three islands – but here are some of the best. Just ask your dive operator or other divers about these and other sites and you can plan your dives.

West Bay

Bonnie's Arch: minimum depth 12 m (40 ft); maximum depth 21 m (70 ft).
Little Tunnels and Chain Reef: minimum depth 20 m (65 ft); maximum depth 30 m (100 ft)
Orange Canyon: minimum depth 18 m (60 ft); maximum depth 30 m (100 ft)
Big Tunnel: minimum depth 25 m (80 ft); maximum depth 37 m (120 ft) – a pair of tunnels discovered in 1970, one of which is at 33 m (110 ft)
Fisheye Fantasy: minimum depth 18 m (60 ft); maximum depth 30 m (100 ft)
Easy Street and In Between: minimum depth 15 m (50 ft); maximum depth 30 m (100 ft)
Neptune's Wall: minimum depth 20 m (65 ft); maximum depth 30 m (100 ft)

Doc Poulson Wreck: minimum depth 12 m (40 ft); maximum depth 15 m (50 ft) – an anchor barge sunk in 1991 as a wreck site and named after Dr Poulson in honour of his work at the recompression chamber at the hospital

Eagle Ray Rock: minimum depth 18 m (60 ft); maximum depth 30 m (100 ft) – an 'L'-shaped canyon with orange sponges and black coral

Slaughterhouse Reef and Wall: minimum depth 12 m (40 ft); maximum depth 14 m (50 ft)

Lost Treasure Reef: minimum depth 13 m (40 ft); maximum depth 15 m (50 ft)

Spanish Anchor: minimum depth 13 m (40 ft); maximum depth 15 m (50 ft)

Paradise Reef: minimum depth 12 m (40 ft); maximum depth 15 m (50 ft)

Dragon's Hole: minimum depth 20 m (65 ft); maximum depth 30 m (100 ft) – a narrow tunnel that is 10 m (35 ft) long and entered at a depth of 20 m (65 ft). It is very dark when you first enter.

Oro Verde Wreck: minimum depth 13 m (40 ft); maximum depth 17 m (55 ft) – the first man-made dive site located where the *Oro Verde* sunk on 31 May 1980

Pageant Beach Reef (the Wharf): minimum depth 13 m (40 ft); maximum depth 15 m (50ft)

LCM David Nicholson Wreck: minimum depth 15 m (50 ft); maximum depth 18 m (60 ft) – a former World War I landing craft that travelled between Little Cayman and Cayman Brac, sunk in 1998 and formed into a dive site

Soto's Cheeseburger: minimum depth 2 m (5 ft); maximum depth 16 m (55 ft) – name comes from its proximity to Burger King in town

Kirk Pride Wreck: maximum depth 242 m (800 ft) – located where the *Kirk Pride* sank on 9 January 1976, it is a fantastic wall dive

Balboa: minimum depth 8 m (30 ft) – the *Balboa* was a 115 m lumber steamer wrecked off George Town during the 1932 hurricane. It was blown up in 1957 and this dive is an exploration wreckage spread over a wide area.

Devil's Grotto: minimum depth 6 m (13 ft)

Seaview Reef: minimum depth 10 m (35 ft); maximum depth 14 m (50 ft) – features bronze mermaid Amphitrite put here by Cathy Church in November 2000. The 10-foot tall figures weighs over 600 lbs.

South Shore

Big Pinnacle: minimum depth 25 m (80 ft); maximum depth 30 m (100 ft) – huge coral pinnacles covered with black coral and barrel sponges, the shallowest being at a depth of 21 m (70 ft)

Palace Wreck Reef: minimum depth 6m (20 ft); maximum depth 15 m (50 ft) – a Norwegian steel-hulled brigantine sunk when it hit a reef in 1903

3D (Dangerous Dan drop off): minimum depth 20 m (65 ft); maximum depth 30 m (100 ft) – large coral buttresses with ravines and underhanging coral gardens

Pedro's Reef: minimum depth 14 m (45 ft); maximum depth 20 m (65 ft) – opposite Pedro Castle

Bats Cave reef: minimum depth 10 m (35 ft) maximum depth 15 m (50 ft) – opposite Coral Cay condominiums

Wahoo wall: minimum depth 20 m (65 ft); maximum depth 30 m (100 ft) – opposite the Lighthouse restaurant

Lost Valley: minimum depth 25 m (80 ft); maximum depth 30 m (100 ft) – opposite Panorama Vista Estates and has canyons and buttresses

East End

The Maze: minimum depth 20 m (65 ft); maximum depth 30 m (100 ft) – many swim-throughs and caves with resident bull sharks and there are pinnacles of brain coral and coral fans here

Grouper Grotto: minimum depth 15 m (50 ft); maximum depth 20 m (65 ft) – many caves, ant tunnels and coral blocks which also have caves

Ridgefield Reef: minimum depth 15 m (50 ft); maximum depth 18 m (60 ft) – the site of a Liberian freighter, built as a liberty ship in Maine 1943, which ran aground in December 1962

Babylon: minimum depth 15 m (50 ft); maximum depth 30 m (100 ft) – west of Old Man Bay with lots of black coral and long, coloured rope sponges

Snapper Hole: minimum depth 10 m (35 ft) – opposite Morrits Tortuga Club with large caves and fissures in the reef. There are many tarpon and an old anchor and ring encrusted with coral. It is a protected site for breeding snapper and grouper.

Two Wrecks: minimum depth 4 m (10 ft); maximum depth 12 m (40 ft) – opposite Morrits Tortuga comprising two wrecks, one on top of the other, namely that of the *Mary Belle*, a steel steamship and the *Methusland steall*, a sailing boat with three masts, a chain and an anchor.

Cinderella's Castle: minimum depth 10 m (35 ft); maximum depth 18 m (60 ft) – many caves and ravines

Shark Alley: minimum depth 14 m (45 ft); maximum depth 16 m (55 ft) – a small chum ball put on the sea bed which attracts 6–9 sharks

North Wall

Turtle Pass: minimum depth 20 m (65 ft); maximum depth 30 m (100 ft) – a small tunnel starts on the sand plain and becomes a fissure with caves on the wall. Good chance to see turtles.

Black Rock Canyon: minimum depth 20 m (65 ft); maximum depth 30 m (100 ft) – a wall with steep fissures.

Valley of the Dolls: minimum depth 20 m (65 ft); maximum depth 30 m (100 ft) – a vertical reef plunging into the depths

White Stroke Canyon: minimum depth 15 m (50 ft); maximum depth 20 m (65 ft) – the reef formations look like exclamation marks when viewed from above which is why this dive has this name

Pinnacle Reef: minimum depth 8 m (30 ft); maximum depth 13 m (40 ft) – coral pinnacles here rise from 13 m (40 ft) to near the surface. There is also a swim-through.

Queen's Throne: minimum depth 5 m (15 ft); maximum depth 15 m (50 ft) – a low wall where there are coral pinnacles which rise to within 5 m of the surface

Haunted House: minimum depth 21 m (70 ft); maximum depth 30 m (100 ft) – two coral columns 50 m (165 ft) apart forming the opening of a large amphitheatre indented into the reef. Black coral trees and large black barrel sponges may be found.

Gail's Mountain: minimum depth 15 m (50 ft); maximum depth 20 m (65ft) – the top of the mountain is about 17 m (56 ft) high and looks like a pyramid. It has good coral and sponges.

Dream Weaver Reef: minimum depth 16 m (55 ft); maximum depth 23 m (75 ft) – this section of the North Wall has coral pinnacles on the reef and there is a tunnel at the top and some swim-throughs

Valley of the Rays: minimum depth 18 m (60 ft); maximum depth 30 m (100 ft) – a good possibility of seeing rays

Little Tunnels: minimum depth 8 m (30 ft); maximum depth 20 m (65 ft)

Hepp's Pipeline: minimum depth 10 m (35 ft); maximum depth 20 m (65 ft)

If you need further information, visit the Cayman Islands Tourist Board's official website specialising in diving www.divecayman.ky or read the *Globetrotter Dive Guide to the Cayman Islands* by Lawson Wood. This gives a listing of all the best dive sites on all three Islands. Cathy Church's photographic book *My Underwater Photo Journey* has fantastic underwater photos of Cayman and from her travels throughout the world's best reefs.

WEDDINGS

The Cayman Islands are an ideal place for a wedding and honeymoon rolled into one. There are many glamorous restaurants for the actual wedding day to choose from and many activities for the wedding party, such as trips to Stingray City and horseback riding. The sandy white beaches, the turquoise sea and the incredible light are all great for wedding pictures.

You can be married in church or in a choice of many outdoor locations – Seven Mile Beach, Pedro St James, Queen Elizabeth II Botanic Park, Cayman Kai, West Bay public dock, Smith Cove, the Bluff or the Heritage House on Cayman Brac, or Point O Sand Beach or Owen Island on Little Cayman. Rings can be bought on the Island duty free and you can organise your wedding in advance or at short notice. From August to November weddings are cheaper as hotels offer special discounts and rates.

Apply for your wedding licence at the Deputy Chief Secretary's Office, tel 244 2222. The District Administration Office handles applications for Cayman Brac and Little Cayman, tel 948 2222. Phoning for an appointment usually means that processing will take half an hour. The documents required as proof of identity are your birth certificate or passport, a Cayman Islands' international embarkation/disembarkation card or a ship's boarding pass and certified or original copies of divorce decrees or death certificates. A charge is made to cover the cost of the licence fee and a postage stamp. The licence must be produced to the marriage officer and is void if not presented within three months.

The wedding has to be attended by a marriage officer and two witnesses and must take place between 06.00 and 20.00.

Picture This, tel 943 3686 or www.picturethis.ky, is a photographic gallery run by Rebecca Davidson and is the best on the island for wedding photography.

REAL ESTATE AND DEVELOPMENT

The Ritz Carlton

The Ritz Carlton is a building of very high quality with fine interiors. It opened in December 2006 and marks another turning point in the development of Cayman. Wherever possible, building is becoming more luxurious with a glossier finish. Some of the best examples are Joe Imperato's Caribbean Club, the Water's Edge and the newly constructed Waterland on the site of the Beach Club Colony right next to the Hyatt. Since the introduction of more hurricane-proof building techniques, more and more developers are attracted to the Cayman Islands. Cayman is an ideal getaway playground for the US – Miami is only a 30- minute flight away. It is also one of the main financial centres so that supports this development.

▲ The Ritz on Seven Mile Beach

Even though the standard of building design and their interiors is very high and very luxurious, some worry about the amount of concrete rising on Seven Mile Beach and the number of fast food chains and shopping malls. There are many who are trying to redress the balance by providing craft markets, views of the heritage of the Cayman Islands and increasing the amount of calypso and reggae playing on the radio. Cayman has become a little piece of America

▲ The Meridian

with the Hard Rock Café and Harley Davidson right in town. Maybe one answer is to ask every investor to make a heritage donation so that as new development takes place, there are more funds to carry on the protection of the Cayman's natural world and historical buildings and the cataloguing of the historical character and heritage of the Island. Many projects have already happened and substantial work is being done on restoring the National Museum on the waterfront. The National Gallery is due to have a new home on the bypass, on land donated by Helen Harquail.

As soon as you head east and enter Bodden Town, Breakers, East End and North Side, you arrive in a different world – nearer to the world that Caymanians used to live in before tourism and financial wands transformed George Town and the West Bay Road. The surrounding areas still have empty beaches with coconut trees and sea birds. Hopefully this will remain unspoilt.

▲ Pink picnic table, North Side

▲ North Side Beach

The Cayman Islands attract as many conservationists as fast, forward-thinking businessmen, so they will maintain a balance between a cosmopolitan, modern island and its historical character and natural beauty.

Ivan (11–12 September 2004)

There are four main books charting this most terrible of storms ever to hit the Cayman Islands. They chart what the islands, as *Paradise Interrupted* explains 'experienced as a community and a hope for restoring a better more improved Cayman'. They also serve as a 'reminder to all who live in harm's way to prepare properly for the next big storm.'

Paradise Interrupted by Joanna Lawrence, photography by Courtney Platt
Ivan: the Full Story by Dominic Tonner
Hurricane Stories by Terri Merren. This is a series of true stories as told by people who directly experienced the storm.
Spirit of Cayman by Sheree Ebanks/Karie Bergstrom

These can all be obtained from the Book Nook in Galleria Plaza and their other branch in George Town.

▲ South Sound after Ivan

Hotels and resorts

George Town and Seven Mile Beach

Many condos such as the Coral Stone Club, The Sovereign, Island Pine, Silver Sands, Developer Brian E Butler's, The Meridian, Colonial Club, Beachcomber, Renaissance and South Bay Beach Club are available along Seven Mile Beach. Joe Imperato's Caribbean Club offers luxurious accommodation, again directly on Seven Mile Beach, and also has one of the best restaurants on the island – the very chic Luca. The Beach Club Colony is now in the process of being knocked down and developed Into Waterland. It is owned by the same people as Water's Edge and will be, similarly, top of the range luxury beachside properties.

Sunset House

Tel: 345 949 7111
www.sunsethouse.com
Situated at the water's edge and marked by a statue of the mermaid Amphitrite, this 57-room hotel offers shore diving, custom boats to Nitrox, the Cathy Church Photographic Centre, My Bar and the Sea Harvest restaurant.

Eldemire's Guest House

Off South Church Street near to Sunset House, this guest house is great for families on a budget, or students. It boasts a very friendly service and has a pool, a barbeque area and a garden. You can choose from four rooms that share a kitchen, sitting room and dining room

▲ The Caribbean Club

or from three other self-contained apartments. It is situated near to Smith Cove and your stay includes a trip to Stingray City on *Sun Rayz*, a Foster's boat that leaves from Safe Haven.

Coral Sands Resort
Tel: 345 949 4400
www.coralsands.ky
This resort comprises 12 ensuite, two-bedroomed units with spacious living and dining room areas, kitchens and poolside or ocean views. It is situated on the outskirts of George Town, seven miles from the centre.

Coral Stone Club
Tel: 345 945 5820
www.coralstoneclub.com
This comprises three-bedroom/three-bathroom condominiums, and an infinity pool and is situated right on Seven Mile Beach.

Treasure Island Resort
Tel: 800 992 2015
www.treasureislandresort.net
This offers 278 guest rooms with a private patio or balcony and a restaurant.

Caribbean Club Seven Mile Beach
Tel: 928 6449
www.caribclub.com
This is described on its website as your 'ultimate Caribbean escape', and they would be right. Here are 37 beautifully appointed and designed three-bedroom/three-bathroom condominiums, all of which have fantastic views from balconies overlooking Seven Mile Beach. It is like a hotel as it has an amazing beach front, a swimming pool, maid service, 24-hours concierge and a world class restaurant – Luca (see restaurant guide, page 116). This is true luxury.

Grand Cayman Marriott Beach Resort
Tel: 345 949 0088
www.marriottgrandcayman.com
This is a 305-room resort on Seven Mile Beach near the George Town end. It offers good restaurants and bars and is the base for Red Sail Sports.

Ritz Carlton
Tel: 345 943 9000
www.ritzcarlton.com
This hotel comprises 365 guestrooms, five restaurants including the Blue Periwinkle, a tennis centre designed by Nick Bollettieri, the ambassadors of the environment family programme devised by Jean-Michel Cousteau, Blue Tip – a nine hole golf course designed by Greg Norman and Silver Rain – the only La Prairie spa in the Caribbean.

▲ Villas of the Galleon

▲ Westin Casuarina

▼ The Courtyard by Marriott

Villas of the Galleon

Tel: 945 4433

www.villasofthegalleon.com

This is a distinctive, one, two and three-bedroom condo. It is a development of white buildings with ultramarine blue roofs. We stayed at room 23, a ground floor, two-bedroom apartment. All the rooms are air-conditioned and beautifully furnished with an amazing view from the living room and master bedroom of the lovely gardens and Seven Mile Beach. The kitchens are well equipped with good glasses, plates cutlery etc. You can barbeque on the beach. The on-site management organises tours if you wish.

Westin Casuarina Resort

Tel: 345 945 3800

www.westincasuarina.net

This has 343 rooms, tropical gardens with waterfalls, fountains, freshwater pools, whirlpools, restaurants, a swim-up pool bar, and Hibiscus, the luxury spa. Avis car rental is available on site.

Comfort Suites

Tel: 345 945 7300

www.caymancomfort.com

This offers three-star accommodation at Seven Mile Beach. All suites have kitchenettes and free internet connection. Here you will find Stinger's poolside restaurant, a jacuzzi and Don Foster's Scuba Centre.

Hyatt Regency Beach Suites

Tel: 345 949 1234

www.hyattregencygrandcayman.com

Situated on Seven Mile Beach, this comprises 53 luxurious suites, two pools, a swim-up bar, a golf course designed by Jack Nicklaus, a fitness centre, dive and other watersports operations and three restaurants.

▲ Seven Mile Beach

Britannia Villas
Tel: 345 945 4144
Penny Cumber at reservations@caymanvillas.com
This offers two-bedroom condos on the Brittania Golf Course, each with a view of the golf course. You may also use the facilities of the nearby Hyatt.

Villa Positano
Tel: 345 945 4144
Penny Cumber at reservations@caymanvillas.com
This is a deluxe, four-bedroom Mediterranean-style home. All rooms have a magnificent view over the Caribbean Sea and the beach. It is situated near Seven Mile Beach.

Courtyard by Marriott
Tel: 345 946 4433
www.marriott.com/gcmcy
This is located on both sides of the road at Seven Mile Beach. Here you will find the Sea Grape Café and, nearby, Red Sail Sports and the Mangrove Grille restaurant. The hotel offers wireless internet and great service. You may rent a car from Avis car rental.

Grand Caymanian Resort
Tel: 345 949 3100
www.grandcaymanian.ky
Situated on North Sound this resort comprises five-star rooms and one and two-bedroom villas. Check www.camanabay.com or tel: 946 2229 for progress of this whole new town built stretching from North Sound across the West Bay Road by Royal Palms with residences on Seven Mile Beach. The architects are Moore, Rubell, Yudel and the landscape architects, Olin Partnership. There will be restaurants, art galleries and department stores, all continuing Cayman's development as a truly upmarket luxury holiday destination.

Island Pine Villas
www.islandpinevillas.com
On Seven Mile Beach, these villas are across the road from the West Shore Centre on West Bay Road.

Crescent Point
Tel: 345 945 2243
www.crescentpoint.com
This comprises 27 three-bedroom villas in a private setting on Seven Mile Beach, a sculptured, free-form, oceanside pool and jacuzzi and tropical gardens.

Rest of Grand Cayman
Cobalt Coast Dive Resort
Tel: 345 946 5656
www.cobaltcoast.com

▲ The Dive Shop at Cobalt Coast Dive Resort

Located on Sea Fan Drive in West Bay, this is an ultra modern, ocean-front resort with one-bedroom suites and guestrooms, a jacuzzi and freshwater pool, a pool deck and a 120-foot dock. There is an on-site dive service operator – Dive Tech. The resort also offers free, wi-fi, high speed internet connection.

Turtle Nest Inn
Tel: 345 947 8665
www.turtlenestinn.com
This is a quiet, peaceful, country inn in Bodden Town and offers very reasonable rates.

◀ Turtle Nest Inn

Reef Resort
Tel: 345 947 3100
www.thereef.com
The Reef Resort at East End has 110 beachfront suites. It has a great beach and fantastic diving and snorkelling facilities, including organised trips to Stingray City. At the restaurant, Castro's Hideaway, the Island-famous Barefoot Man entertains you with his calypso on Tuesdays and Thursdays.

▲ The Barefoot Man performs on Tuesdays and Thursdays at the Reef

SPEEDWAY PUBLIC LIBRARY, SPEEDWAY, INDIANA

Morritt's Grand Resort
Tel: 345 947 7449
www.morritts.com

Cayman Castle East End
Tel: 804 934 0666
www.caymancastle.com
This is an amazing castle right by the Police Station in East End, with fantastic views, an infinity pool and a beach. It comprises a four-bedroom castle and a two-bedroom guest house, each with separate pools. Rooms can be rented individually.

▲ Cayman Castle

Compass Point Dive Resort
Tel: 345 947 7500
www.compasspoint.ky
In a tranquil setting, this resort offers 18 one and two-bedroom condominiums with a private patio or balcony overlooking the Caribbean Sea. Ocean Frontiers, the on-site dive operator offer the adventure of some fantastic diving.

Retreat at Rum Point
Tel: 866 947 9135
www.grandcaymanretreat.com
This offers two and three-bedroom condominiums with a pool, a sandy beach, ocean views and a quiet North Side location right near to Rum Point. It also has a beach bar and grill and Red Sail Sports and the Kaibo Yacht Club are just down the road.

Seaspray Too
Tel: 345 945 4144
Penny Cumber reservations@caymanvillas.com
This is a three-bedroom villa near Bodden Town. It is situated on a cliff top and has spectacular ocean views.

The Yellow House
Tel: 345 947 8714
www.northside.ky
This is an ocean-front, modern and fully-equipped house in North Side. It offers three-bedroom accommodation with an ocean-front deck and large balconies. It also offers free broadband, kayak and satellite TV facilities.

The Pink House
Tel: 345 945 4144
Penny Cumber reservations@caymanvillas.com
This is a three-bedroom, beachfront home in North Side with views of the Caribbean Sea.

Beachplum Villa
Tel: 862 881 4099
www.beachplumvilla.com
This is a newly-constructed two-storey home four miles from Rum Point, with a freshwater swimming pool in North Side. Chisholm's Grocery store is a two-minute walk away.

Far Tortuga
www.fartortuga.com
This is a luxury, beachfront villa in North Side with a studio cottage. It has spectacular views and is near to Rum Point and Kaibo Beach Bar.

Barefoot Kai
Tel: 345 945 4144
Penny Cumber reservations@caymanvillas.com
This is a three-bedroom Cayman Kai home situated on the shallow, calm cove.

Kaiconut
Tel: 345 945 4144
Penny Cumber reservations@caymanvillas.com
This is a four-bedroom house in Cayman Kai.

Coconut Beach
Tel: 345 945 4144
Penny Cumber reservations@caymanvillas.com
This is a four-bedroom, beachfront villa on the beach in North Side.

Coral Reef
Tel: 345 945 4144
Penny Cumber reservations@caymanvillas.com
This is a spacious, four-bedroom, beachfront villa on Seven Mile Beach. It is near to George Town, shopping, watersports, golf courses and restaurants.

Villa Zara
Tel: 345 945 3617
www.rentalsincayman.ky
This is a four-bedroom villa in Cayman Kai (in my book, the pale olive one) with spectacular views. It has marble flooring, a gourmet kitchen and antique furnishings and an on-site chef and concierge service is available.

OchKai
Tel: 345 945 4144
www.caymanislands.com
This is a four-bedroom house in Cayman Kai with its own private pool and a bar area on the beach for barbecues and private sunbathing.

Gardens of the Kai
Tel: 345 947 9266
www.caymankai.com
This comprises a selection of one, two and three-bedroom guest houses all located directly on the beach in Cayman Kai.

Grand Cayman Haven
Tel: 612 817 4200
www.grandcaymanhaven.com
This is a one-bedroom condo at Kaibo Yacht Club.

Coconut Bay
Tel: 345 929 9622
www.caymanvacation.info
This is a selection of three-bedroom, luxury townhouses set in tropical gardens and with two pools on the north-west point of the Island. It offers very good diving.

Villa Bellagio
Tel: 345 916 0318
www.villabellagiocayman.com
Right on the beach, this yellow house offers eight beds within its five-bedroom accommodation.

Cayman Villas, tel 345 945 4144 or www.caymanvillas.com, are the best company to contact to book beachfront condos and villas. They have properties on Seven Mile Beach, at South Sound, East End, Cayman Kai and North Side as well as on Little Cayman and Cayman Brac. To make a reservation, contact Penny Cumber reservations@caymanvillas.com.

RESTAURANTS
There are so many restaurants on Cayman that it would be impossible to cover them all here, but pick up a copy of **Good Taste**, Cayman's definitive dining and entertainment guide published by Charles Grover and Joanna Boxall for a full listing of addresses and phone numbers. This magazine is brilliantly produced and is complete with sample menus and a bar and bartender guide.

You can also order through the Fine Dine-in delivery service from over 30 top restaurants, tel 949 3463 or www.finedinein.com.

Local Caymanian food
Jerk chicken is found in many roadside cafés and is made by marinading chicken in a mixture of thyme, allspice, pimento and scotch bonnet peppers and then served with a hot sauce. Other Caymanian dishes include conch stew, local steam fish, jerk pork, fried chicken, rice and peas, plantain, fritters, chicken or fish soup, curry goat, oxtail and cow foot. All these give you a real taste of Cayman. Other dishes are the typically Caribbean ackee and codfish, and green banana and

dumpling. At the **East End Fish Fry**, Captain Herman serves up his own catches of red snapper, barracuda, tuna, mahi mahi, and wahoo, accompanied by fritters, onions and scotch bonnet sauce on picnic tables right by the beach. **Turtle stew**, historically a mainstay of the Caymanian diet, is seasoned with hot peppers, coconut, onions and spices. In the old days, Caymanians also ate lobster, conch, whelks, yellowtail and turbot. Christmas traditionally was a time for beef, which was a real treat.

▲ Chester's Jerk Centre, Pease Bay

Fish rundown is another traditional dish made by cutting turbot or red snapper into large chunks. Slits are then cut in the chunks and they are marinaded in chopped-up onions, country peppers, scallions, scotch bonnet peppers and lime juice. When this is cooked, coconut milk and grated pumpkin are added to the pot. Dumplings are made by grating pumpkin or cornmeal, which is mixed with flour and baking powder and then rolled into balls. These are added to the pot for 20 minutes. Sometimes, the rundown contains breadfruit and green banana. **Fish Tea** is made by using similar ingredients and is of the same consistency as gravy. **Heavy Cake** is made by boiling coconut with nutmeg, cinnamon, vanilla, butter and sugar, then mixing it with yam, cassava or pumpkin. This mixture is then baked. The recipes haven't changed for over 100 years, and all the ingredients come from the Caymanian ground.

Local Caymanian restaurants

Seymour's Jerk Centre
Shedden Road
Tel: 916 8531

Singh's Roti Shop, Restaurant and Bar
Shedden Road
Tel: 946 7684

Rankin's Jerk Centre
Bodden Town
Tel: 947 3155

Harry's Caribbean Bar & Grill
Tel: 945 2025

Mango Tree
Tel: 949 0732

Heritage Kitchen
Turn left at the West Bay four-way stop and go down Boggy Sand Road for fish tea, fish rundown, barbecue chicken and ribs, snapper and mahi mahi.

Chef John's Barbecue Stall
West Bay Dock for ribs, chicken and steak – all cooked on hot coals.

Lorna's Jerk Centre and Biggie's Jerk Centre
Bodden Town

Chester's
This is the bright orange building just past Bodden Town in Pease Bay

Wood's Jerk Centre
This is right next to Chester's.

North Side Fish Fry
This is next to the Over the Edge Café.

Vivine's Kitchen
East End

Willie's fresh fruit juices stall is in Red Bay, just before Grand Harbour, and serves juices, coconut water, shakes, cakes, tarts, jams and jellies. All the ingredients are supplied by Whistling Duck Farm, North Side which grows tomatoes, star apples, papayas, naseberries, guavas, pineapples, soursops and starfruit. The company, owned by Willie Ebanks, also makes mango chutney, orange pepper jelly and stewed papaya. Willie's son, George, is often at the van and his great-aunt Nell makes thatchwork baskets, fans and hats which are also for sale. His mother, Zelma-Lee, makes the jams and jellies and the cassava, pumpkin or plantain cakes.

Supermarkets
Fosters Food Fair, Kirk Supermarket and Hurley's

George Town
Grand Old House
South Church Street
Tel: 949 9333

This is luxury at its best – sea bass with lobster ravioli, asparagus, champagne sauce and caviar – wines, champagne, brandy, liqueurs, cocktails – all served in a beautiful chandeliered bar. Here you can eat inside in the dining room or outside on the terrace. The night we went, a Cuban cigar maker was on site. The restaurant offers a wonderful service and, even though very grand, the management is great with kids. Look out for plates that you can buy and take home as souvenirs.

▲ Grand Old House

My Bar/Sea Harvest
Sunset House
South Church Street
Tel: 949 7111
This is at Cathy Church's hotel for divers.

Jolly Roger and Anne Bonny
dinner cruises
Tel: 945 7245

Hard Rock Café
South Church Street
Tel: 945 2020**Paradise Bar & Grill**
Tel: 945 1444
Pina coladas, mudslides, Cayman Islands iced teas, lemonades, beers, liqueurs and the usual happy hour prices. Friday at 17.00 is normally the most popular time to come here. It offers a contemporary, international cuisine and is a cruise ship haunt right by Eden Rock which is good for snorkelling.

▲ The view from Paradise Bar

Brasserie
Cricket Square off Elgin Avenue
Tel: 945 1815
'Think Global – Eat Local'. This is very chic with a completely unique menu. The restaurant is right in the middle of George Town and is very popular with British expatriates.

▲ The Brasserie

Breadfruit Tree Garden Restaurant
Eastern Avenue
Tel: 928 8990
Local Caribbean cuisine

Champion House and Champion House II
George Town
Tel: 949 7882
This offers local Caribbean cuisine including conch stew, cayman-style chicken or fish, cowfoot, ackee and codfish. It was first opened in 1965, so is a Caymanian institution.

Mango Tree
Shedden Road, near the airport
Tel: 949 0723
This is the largest Caribbean restaurant on the Island, with a Cuban/Latin feel. It is good for Chicharron – sliced fried pork meat with crackling accompanied by fried plantains and breadfruit. It offers Cuban cocktails: mojitos, daiquiris and cuba libres. The locals play dominoes here and there are three parrots, ten iguanas, tropical fish and turtles.

Harry's Caribbean Bar and Grill
Smith Road
Tel: 945 2025

Macdonalds (not the fast food variety)
Shedden Road
Tel: 949 4640
This is one of Cayman's oldest restaurants for burgers, fry chicken and seafood.

China Village
North Sound Way
Tel: 945 3490
Chinese food

Silver spoon
Tel: 945 4504
Indian and Pakistani food

Bayside Café
Tel: 946 2482
This is an Indian restaurant with a view of the harbour. The Head chef is Angelo from Goa who has lived in Cayman since 1991.

Hammerheads
Tel: 949 3080
This is excellent for views of the sunset.

Lobster Pot
Waterfront
North Church Street
Tel: 949 2736
This is Cayman's longest-established steak and seafood restaurant as it has been here for 40 years. It offers spectacular views.

Señor Frogs
Tel: 946 3764
This offers Mexican cuisine and is a completely mad, cruise ship haunt – a clown blows up balloon hats and there is lots of loud entertainment.

▲ The clown makes balloon hats at Señor Frogs

Guy Harvey's Island Grill
Tel: 946 9000
This offers French cuisine and excellent seafood with views over George Town's picturesque harbour. The walls show a collection of work by the marine wildlife artist Guy Harvey who also owns the gallery downstairs.

▲ Guy Harvey's Island Grill

Rackham's Pub
Tel: 945 3860

Jimmy Buffet's Margaritaville
With restaurants in Jamaica and the Turks & Caicos Islands, this serves up hamburgers, tortillas and cocktails. It is very popular with the cruise ships and has a DJ, entertainment and a fantastic spiral water slide and pool overlooking George Town Harbour.

▲ The water slide and pool at Margaritaville

Breezes by the Bay
Rhum Deck
Tel: 943 8439
This offers beautiful views of George Town Harbour, typical Caribbean food – the shrimp and samosas are excellent.

Great Wall
Tel: 947 8888
Chinese food.

Ye Olde English Bakery
Mary Street
Tel: 945 2420
This is a Coffee Shop and bakery.

Casanova
North Church Street
Tel: 949 7633
This offers Italian food on the Waterfront.

Bacchus
Fort Street
George Town
Tel: 949 5747
Englishman Keith Griffin is chef here.

West Bay Road

The Wharf

Tel: 949 2231

This has a huge verandah which overlooks the Caribbean Sea. You can eat in the dining room or on the seaside patio at night. The tarpon feeding time is 21.00. The Wharf also holds salsa nights and monthly 70s discos.

Stax Restaurant & Bar

West Shore Centre

Tel: 945 7829

This offers contemporary American food, including soups, salads, wraps, burgers, steak and seafood.

Thai Orchid

Queens Court Plaza

West Bay Road

Tel: 949 7922

This offers Thai sushi.

Blue and Periwinkle

The Ritz

Tel: 943 9000

The head chef is Eric Ripert, co-owner of Le Bernardin in NYC. Periwinkle is a Mediterranean Grill – they often hold movie nights. Blue is the more formal restaurant specialising in seafood and offers a fixed price, three-course menu. You can also book your own private table in a cabana by the pool or actually book a table in the pool for very romantic dining

▲ Periwinkle at the Ritz

7 Prime Cuts and Sunsets

The Ritz

Tel: 943 9000

This steak house offers a great view. Sunday champagne brunch is available from 11.00–15.00

Triple Crown Pub

opposite The Marriott

Tel: 943 7821

This is a traditional pub with a great menu – smoked salmon mussels, spinach or chicken satay salad, irish stew, roast beef dinner, traditional English fry up, beef and ale pie and shepherd's pie.

▲ Luca at the Caribbean Club

Luca

The Caribbean Club

This offers Italian food and is run by the same owners as Ragazzi on Buckingham Square. Enjoy the Muraka prints on the wall in this newly-built condo development on Seven Mile Beach.

Yoshi Sushi

The Falls Plaza

Tel: 943 9674

This has a very chic and modern interior and offers excellent sushi – make sure you reserve a table.

▲ Private and romantic, poolside dining at the Ritz

Myrtle's
Queens Court Plaza
Tel: 949 7868
This is the only place serving genuine Caymanian and Caribbean dishes, including very good jerk chicken, pork, fish, shrimp and steak.

Stingers
Seven Mile Beach
Tel: 945 3000
This offers a poolside restaurant and bar in a garden. It is popular with the locals. Dishes include conch chowder, burgers, ribs and linguini.

Deckers
opposite the Hyatt
Tel: 945 6600
This offers Meditteranean fusion cuisine. There is a double-decker bus outside which is the bar.

Mezza
Seven Mile Beach
Tel: 946 3992
This offers Mediterranean cuisine and an international gourmet menu.

Neptune
Trafalgar Square
Tel: 946 8709
This offers Italian continental food. The owners are Yunio Lopez and chef Raj Kumar.

Reef Grill
Royal Palms
Tel: 945 6358
This offers contemporary American dishes. During the day, try Royal Palms the beach bar for burgers, sandwiches and salads and great cocktails by Seven Mile Beach.

Hemmingway's and Bamboo
The Hyatt
Tel: 945 5700

Blue Iguana Grill
Safe Haven
Crystal Harbour
Tel: 949 3100
This offers international and Caribbean food at the Grand Caymanian Resort.

Chicken Chicken
West Shore Centre
Tel: 945 2290
This offers Caribbean wood-roasted chicken.

Calico Jack's
This is right on Seven Mile Beach by the Public Beach on West Bay Road. It offers great cocktails, conch fritters and prawn or chicken salads. It is perfect both for lunch, so you can have an afternoon swim, or for dinner after you have watched the stunning sunset.

▲ Calico Jack's

Cimboco Caribbean Café
near the Marquee cinema
Tel: 947 2782
Named after Cayman's first motorised boat, launched in May 1927 by the Cayman Islands Motor Boat Company this offers fresh Caribbean food and home-made ice cream.

Eats Café
opposite the Westin
West Bay Road
Tel: 943 3287
This is a modern American diner offering great breakfasts and burgers, fajitas, stir fries quesadillas and great sandwiches for lunch. There are very long queues at the weekends as it is also a favourite with the locals.

Bed
Treasure Island Hotel
Tel: 949 7199
This offers Glbla asian inspired fusion food. There is an extremely chic bar here with velvet sofas. Try to book a booth – they all have golden organza curtains for privacy. The menus are red and purple velvet and the waiters wear silk pyjamas – all is about comfort and luxury and the food is some of the best on the island, including excellent duck wraps, lobster thermidore and delicious desserts. The service here is fantastic.

▲ The booths at Bed

▲ Lobster Thermidore at Bed

Ernestos
Strand Plaza
Tel: 945 3109
This offers Latin cuisine in an elegant interior. There is an excellent bar and cigar lounge.

Ragazzi
Buckingham Square
Tel: 945 3484
This is run by Paolo Polloni and Andi Marcher and the head chef is Federico Destro. Polloni and Marcher have now opened a new restaurant at the Caribbean Club called Luca. They offer the best pizzas – try Arugula with parma ham, goats cheese and arugula or sautéed lobster penne.

Full of Beans
Pasadora Place
Tel: 943 2326
The mosaic mirror and vintage wooden tables makes for an eclectic atmosphere here. It offers waffles, wraps, paninis, great coffees and often has art exhibitions.

Edoardo's
Coconut Place
Tel: 945 4408
This offers incredible old fashioned Italian cooking.

Aqua Beach
across from The Marriot
Tel: 949 8498

Pirates Den (P.D.s pub)
Galleria Plaza
Tel: 949 7144

Ferdinand's
The Westin
Tel: 945 3800

Mangrove Grill
The Marriott Courtyard
Tel: 946 4433
This offers international and Caribbean dishes.

Casa Havana
The Westin
Tel: 945 3800
This offers four-diamond rated, very posh, very formal, but excellent world-class food. It is definitely worth booking a table for that very special, unforgettable meal. They have stingray shaped butter.

▲ The bar at Casa Havana at the Westin Casuarina Resort

Lone Star
opposite The Hyatt
Tel: 945 5175
This has Tex Mex. Traditional American Sports Bar with 26 televisions – a great party place as well.

Copper Falls Steakhouse
Canal Point Drive
Tel: 945 4755 43
This offers a unique menu from which you can choose five starches – including garlic mashed potato, rice pilaf or linguini – three vegetables and six steak sauces to accompany certified Angus beef steaks. Your first drink is included in the price.

Abacus
Camana Bay
This is run by Neil and Markus of Deckers.

More restaurants are due to open in Camana Bay by the end of 2008. Check www. camanabay.com for details.

West Bay
Cracked Conch
beside the Turtle Farm
Tel: 945 5217

▲ The terrace at the Cracked Conch

This offers Caribbean Fusion. It is very romantic here at night and is absolutely fabulous for lunch on the terrace with a great view over the sea. It also offers a great brunch on Sundays.

▲ The Bar at the Cracked Conch

Calypso Grill
Morgans Harbour
West Bay
Tel: 949 3948
This offers continental seafood in a really wonderful continental atmosphere. You can eat inside or outside on the deck overlooking Morgan's Harbour. The service here is excellent.

Pappagallo
Barker's
West Bay
Tel: 949 1119
This is an Italian and a must! It is one of the most popular restaurants on Grand Cayman and has become a classic. Pappagallo is an incredible thatched building beside a

wetlands lake which is beautifully lit at night. The interior is just as magical. Try and get a table on the right hand side of the bar as you go in with the parrots, housed behind glass and who watch you while you eat. The menu includes delicious seafood, pasta and steaks. The service is excellent. The African Grey parrot at the entrance is called Humphrey Bogart and likes being fed peanuts.

▲ Pappagallo

Cobalt Coast
Sea Fan Drive
West Bay
Tel: 946 5656
Here, breakfast and lunch guests can swim or snorkel off the 120 foot dock or the freshwater pool. It offers international and Caribbean cuisine.

Fisherman's Reef
Morgan's Harbour
West Bay
Tel: 945 5879
The chef here is Ottmar Weber.

Schooners Bar and Grill
Boatswain's Beach
Tel: 945 3894
This offers excellent burritos, caesar salads and delicious smoothies.

Heritage Kitchen
just off Boggy Sand Road
West Bay
Located on the seaward side of the four way stop, this offers fish tea, barbeque chicken and ribs, snapper and mahi mahi.

Chef John's Barbeque Stall
West Bay dock
This offers ribs, steak and chicken, rice and peas served with coleslaw or potato salad.

▲ Schooners Bar and Grill

Rest of the Island

Red Bay Country & Western
Tel: 945 4079
This offers local Caribbean

Dragon Garden
Red Bay Plaza
Tel: 947 1166
This serves Chinese food.

Willie's
Willie's fresh fruit and juices stall just before Grand Harbour as you head towards George Town offers shakes, cakes, tarts, jams and jellies – all made using ingredients grown at the Whistling Duck Farm owned by Willie Ebanks. You may also buy thatchwork items.

Black Pearl Grille
Grand Harbour
This offers great steaks, chicken and burgers.

Lighthouse Restaurant
Tel: 947 2047
This serves local seafood and Italian cuisine. The lighthouse is a local landmark in this beautiful Caymanian village and has been renovated and turned into a beautiful restaurant with superb views over the sea. The head chef is Remy and Captain G and his crew are in charge of service. They have won the award of excellence from the Wine Spectator since 1997.

▲ The Lighthouse Restaurant

Lorna's Jerk Centre and Biggie's Centre
Bodden Town

Chester's Jerk Centre
Savannah

Over the Edge
North Side
Tel: 947 9568
This offers typical Caribbean cuisine. The building is a classic here in North Side – it used to be called 'Apollo 11' which was a very popular bar and restaurant – but it is now even better for lunch or dinner. It is called 'Over the Edge' as the building is literally hanging on stilts over the edge of the sea which is stunning.

North Side Fish Fry
This is located next to the 'Over the Edge' restaurant.

Wreck Bar and Grill
Rum Point
Tel: 947 9412
This offers jerk and fresh fish, chicken and hamburgers and great cocktails, mudslides and pina coladas from 10.00–17.00. It is located on the beach at Rum Point and you will find it is less busy during the week as the locals all come here at the weekends.

Castro's Hideaway
Reef Resort
Tel: 947 3100
This is where the Barefoot Man plays his calypso on Tuesdays and Thursdays. It offers crab cakes, conch, mahi mahi, shrimp and flat iron steak.

Portofino Wreck View
East End
Tel: 947 2700
Italian food.

Burger King, **KFC**, **Pizza Hut**, **Subway**, **Wendy's**, **Domi**no's are all fast food outlets.

Kaibo Bar and Grill
Tel: 947 9975
This offers excellent, inventive, Caribbean
food and an excellent service. It is a great
place to bring the kids for lunch as they can
play by the shallow water on the beach very
near to you while you relax and unwind.

▲ Kaibo Bar and Grill

Vivine's Kitchen
East End
Tel: 947 7435
Local Caymanian food.

BARS AND CLUBS
Evenings in Grand Cayman start at 17.00 – the start of happy hour –
and ends at 03.00 (apart from Saturdays – when it ends at midnight –
and Sundays, when everything is closed). The nightlife is everywhere
and very busy.

The main bars are **Fidel Murphy's**, **My Bar** at Sunset
House, **Coconut Joe's**, **Bed**, **Billy Bones**, **The Wharf**, **Attic**,
Mezza, **Sapphire**, **The Lone Star**, **Deckers** and **Aqua Beach**.

Drinks available include pina coladas, mudslides and any kind
of cocktails, beers, wines and all liqueurs. You will find a wide variety
of music, including reggae, calypso, country, folk, rock and r and b.
Famous DJs are to be found at hotels, bars and nightclubs. From

A waitress at sunset at Calico Jack's bar ▶

▲ KK and band singing at the Westin Bar

Mondays to Fridays, the bars open until 01.00 and clubs close at 03.00. Ask a local about the types of music played at the clubs and on which night, or check the 'get out' update in the Friday edition of *The Caymanian Compass*.

There is a lot of live music in both indoor and outdoor bars which feature different acts all week. Look out for the local band **Ratskin**, and **Chuck and Barrie** at Café Med who play calypso and jazz-style music. **Hi Tide**, who play pop and reggae at Cayman Jazz Fest, perform at Decker's opposite the Hyatt on West Bay Road. **Heat** is a soca, calypso, reggae band. **Gary Ebanks**, the jazz saxophonist and his band **Intransit**, appear at Bamboo the sushi restaurant at the Hyatt. **KK** is a famous singer on the Island who regularly appears at the Jazz Fest and performs at many different locations. The Ritz Carlton features the steel pan player **Earl La Pierre** in the Silver Palm and Periwinkle lounges. **Barefoot Man** is at the Reef Resort in East End every Tuesday and Thursday. He has been playing in Cayman for 30 years and used to play at the old Holiday Inn every night. There is karaoke at Morrit's Tortuga Club, also at East End.

Bob Mosley and his **Gone Country** and **Catch of the Day** bands provide Country and Western which is very popular across the Caribbean at Double D's (otherwise known as Decker's), the Lone Star, Sunshine Suites or Royal Palms. Royal Palms also showcases **Coco Red, Footloose** and **Henry Leslie**. The Wharf has a monthly disco party, **Boogie Nights**, sponsored by Kiss Fm, one of Cayman's radio stations. **Eugenio Leno** plays tableside on his harp here the rest of the week. Make sure you catch **George Davidson**, the pianist at the Westin, while sipping cocktails in their chic bar.

The main night clubs are **Matrix, Pepper's Lounge, Next Level** (opposite the Marriott on Seven Mile Beach)**, District 6**, the **O Bar** at Queens Court Plaza on a Wednesday night after the band at the **Royal Palms** and **Jungle.** Again, check *The Caymanian Compass* for listings of the week's entertainment and to find out the different themed nights.

Look out for the special lounge, Ibiza-style nights at the Ritz Carlton by their North Sound Pool, such as Luna Lounge sponsored by Moet and Chandon and Belvedere Vodka – as the flyers say, 'lounge in poolside Bedouin tents, groove to the beats of far-away places, sip elegant cocktails waterside, socialise under the stars'. These also feature Cayman's famous DJ Alexi. The music is described as 'samba-afro-jazz' and 'elegant beach house'.

Camana Bay is a new town spanning 500 acres between Seven Mile Beach and North Sound. It is a continually-developing project with plans for offices, residential areas, a marina, Island Companies duty free shopping, a 20-acre park, a hotel on Seven Mile Beach and a 75 ft observation tower with views across the island and a floor-to-ceiling mosaic of the Caymans' marine life. Camana Way is the main approach from West Bay Road and care has been taken to landscape with indigenous plants. Already, there is the **Hollywood Theatres**, **Books & Books**, **NKY** stocking the main fashion labels, **Café del Sol** and **Abacus** restaurant. Always check www.camanabay.com for details of events at this vibrant, state-of-the-art, new town.

▼ Camana Bay town centre

❸ CAYMAN BRAC

The Sister Islands of Cayman Brac and Little Cayman remind Caymanians of how Grand Cayman used to be 40 years ago. There is still the possibility that the small islands will host more development but, hopefully, can be home to eco-tourism, focusing on the heritage of the Cayman Islands and educating people about the fragile eco-systems. Attractions are fishing, tranquillity, the natural beauty of the islands, hiking and diving – these are getaway resorts from Grand Cayman's nightlife and shopping.

There are plans to set up a wind turbine company on the Bluff on Cayman Brac – the first mass generation of alternative energy in the Cayman Islands. It is hoped that the Government of the Cayman Islands will support the sister islands as eco-destinations rather than allow them to become developed in the same way as Grand Cayman.

Cayman Brac is 89 miles northeast of Grand Cayman. It is 12 miles long and one mile wide. Its population is 1600. The Brac is still very safe and friendly. There is a completely different atmosphere here to that of Grand Cayman, which is definitely a business capital.

Most of the hotels are just minutes from **Gerard Smith Airport** and it is a very quick drive around the island. If you drive east along the Southside Road West you come to the **Westerly Ponds**. These are two mangrove, salt water ponds which are bird sanctuaries where you can find ducks, egrets, herons and white barn owls. Past the Westerly Ponds is the **Salt Water Pond**. Nearby, look for a sign pointing to **Rebecca's Cave** – this is the grave site of Rebecca Bodden's baby who died in the 1932 storm. The cave was used as the main hurricane shelter.

Cayman Brac has the highest point on all the islands – the Bluff, which is a cliff 144 feet above sea level. The National Trust has created a one-mile nature trail on the bluff and nearby 281-acre Parrot Reserve which was opened in July 1996. Here, as well as the rare Cayman Brac Parrot, you can see frigate birds, brown boobies and peregrine falcons. There are many caves here including **Peter's Cave** and **Halfway Ground Cave**, where bats live and where the Brackers hid during the 1932 storm. These are maintained by the National Trust who has installed guide rails and ladders. New caves appear over the years as the rain water gradually dissolves the rock. There are great views from here and the National Trust organises hikes to see green parrots, soldier crabs and lizards.

▲ The Bluff, Cayman Brac

Nani's cave (the name is carved nearby on a tree trunk) is just below the surface of the Bluff. You have to look carefully for it as the entrance is just a few feet wide. Inside, there are interesting mineral deposits with hundreds of stalactites and stalagmites, some of which have joined together to form natural pillars. Another cave has the appearance of a skull as you look inside. The caves have a certain atmosphere, as it is known that the pirates in the seventeenth and eighteenth centuries used to stop at the Cayman Islands and may have hidden treasure here.

Caves ▶

By the Bluff, at the end of a road, sits a boulder known as **Slaughterhouse** – named after the pirate custom of murdering someone after burying their treasure. On one side of the boulder a small skull has been carved into it. Many young Brackers, including **Tenson Scott**, tried to find treasure in this area. One day, two Brackers went to the spot with a metal detector and found, under a large, flat rock, a chest known now as 'Slaughterhouse Treasure'. The chest contained disintegrating paper money and gold and silver coins.

In 1997, the Cayman Islands' Government funded signed trails on the islands and Foots has developed his **Lost City of Atlantis** as a dive site. This includes many sculptures of buildings and people which is growing into a large underwater community.

▲ Foots and his Lost City of Atlantis – a dive attraction

In Oliviney Dixon's yard there is a different kind of treasure – a 95 lb, titanium-coated ball he found on the beach. This was later identified as a high pressure helium tank used on unmanned Atlas Launch vehicles which probably left Cape Canaveral in April 1994. These vehicles carried NASA satellites to provide weather and solar information and to relay signals from ships and aircraft. This tank floated in the ocean until Oliviney found it on the southern shore of the Brac in 1998.

Pollard Bay is by the Bluff. Further along is **Ashton Reid Road** which leads to the 180-acre **Cayman Brac Parrot Reserve**. Again, the National Trust will organise a hike to explore the area and show you the tall cactus, candlewood, red birch, mahogany and cedar trees.

Stake Bay has a duty free store and Faith Hospital. Here also is the Government Administration Building and the **Cayman Brac Museum**, tel 948 2622, which is open from Monday to Friday, 09.00–16.00 (closed for lunch 12.00–13.00) and on Saturday, 09.00–12.00. This is a white building, with swing seats on its front porch, that became a museum in 1983. It once served as the post office, customs bureau, treasury and bank. The museum houses exhibits of old photographs, wooden radios, hurricane lamps, sewing machines, clothing, crocodile skins, anchors and turtle shells.

Also worth a visit is **Tibbetts Square** which is the island's main shopping and commercial centre. It has a grocery store and a shop called the **Treasure Chest** which sells clothing, jewellery and souvenirs. **Ed's Place** is a restaurant next door.

▲ Town

▲ Church

NIM's (Native Island Made), tel 948 0461, is a small cottage shop owned by Tenson Scott who makes jewellery and small sculptures from Caymanite shells and sea eggs.

▲ Tenson Scott and a slab of Caymanite

The **Columbus Gardens** are beautiful gardens on the Bluff and were planned and created by the Quincentennial Committee. There is a Wall of Honour featuring a carving of Columbus and a list of 500 names of people, past and present, who have contributed significantly to the development of the Sister Islands over the past 500 years. There are boardwalks and a gazebo.

Hotels, apartments, restaurants and dive operators

Divi Tiara
Tel: 948 1553
This offers beachfront rooms with hammocks on the beach.

Brac Reef Beach Resort
Tel: 948 1323
This is the most luxurious hotel on the island and offers 40 beachfront rooms, a restaurant, spa, gym, wireless internet and water sport activities. Dives can be organised from here through Reef Divers, the local dive operation.

Villa Marbella
Tel: 360 877 5414
www.villamarbella.net
This villa has a large sundeck and a private swimming pool surrounded by palms and hammocks right on the beach. You can rent the whole villa for up to 16 people or rent the three units separately. The 'Marinera' has two bedrooms and two bathrooms. The 'Paraiso' has one bedroom and a bathroom. The 'Vista Mar' is a one bedroom apartment.

Walton's Mango Manor and Sea Dreams Villa
Tel: 345 948 2551
www.waltonsmangomanor.com
This offers deluxe rooms with private bathrooms in an elegant, traditional style. It is set in a tropical garden. Sea Dreams Villa is a two-bedroom villa right on the beach and forms part of the resort. If you want to, you can get married in the private chapel or in a gazebo by the sea.

Carib Sands
Tel: 948 1121

Cayman Cottage
Tel: 948 1617

La Esperanza
Tel: 948 0591

Brac Caribbean Beach Village
Tel: 948 2265

Bluff View
Tel: 970 493 5801

Cayman Breakers
Tel: 948 1463

Restaurants

The Palms
Brac Reef Resort
Tel: 948 1323

Captain's Table
Divi Tiara
Tel: 948 1418

Aunt Sha's Kitchen
Tel: 948 1581

La Esperanza
Tel: 948 0531

Dive operators

Divi Tiara
Tel: 948 1553

Reef Divers
Brac Reef Resort
Tel: 948 1642

DIVE SITES

At the **MV Captain Keith Tibetts** – the site of the Russian destroyer which sank in 1996 – you can see eagle rays, stingrays, groupers and angelfish.

The **Lost City of Atlantis** features underwater sculptures by local artist Foots. Little Cayman's Bloody Bay Wall is made up of two walls plunging from a depth of 18 feet to a depth of 6000 feet.

The island is one of the least developed in the Caribbean and boasts some of the most biologically diverse reef systems in the region in which you may find eagle rays, conch, moray eels, sand tile fish, groupers, turtles and the occasional barracuda.

Foots, the artist who created 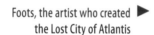 the Lost City of Atlantis

Cayman Brac Public Beach on the south coast, one mile east of Aunt Sha's restaurant, has showers, restrooms and cabanas.

North Shore

Greenhouse Reef – minimum depth 7m (25 ft); maximum depth 15 m (50 ft). Here you will find angelfish and butterflyfish.

Hoyts Wall – minimum depth 20 m (65 ft); maximum depth 30 m (100 ft). This wall is like the Grand Cayman's North Wall.

Snapper Reef – minimum depth 8 m (30 ft); maximum depth 15 m (50 ft).

School House Wall – minimum depth 25 m (80 ft). This has a deep open water drop to the reef.

Kissimmee Wreck – minimum depth 14 m (45 ft); maximum depth 20 m (65 ft). This dive wreck is to be found at the north end of Stake Bay and is the site of a tug boat that was sunk in 1982. The boat is 12 m (40 ft) long and rests upside down.

Garden Eel Wall and Leslyn's Palace – minimum depth 20 m (65 ft); maximum depth 30 m (100 ft). There is a large colony of garden eels at the top of the reef.

Captain Keith Tibbetts Wreck – minimum depth 15 m (50 ft); maximum depth 30 m (100 ft). In 1996, this decommissioned Russian destroyer was sunk off the north shore of Cayman Brac. Built in 1984 in Nakhodka in Russia, it is a brigadier Type II class frigate and is 95 m (330 ft) long and 12.8 m (42.6 ft) wide. It weighs 1590 tons and was, as Patrol Vessel 356, part of the Russian fleet stationed in Cuba during the Cold War. In 1996, the Cayman Islands' Government bought the ship. The location was chosen so as to cause minimal environmental damage. The ship was renamed the MV *Captain Keith Tibbetts* by the wife of the Cayman Islands' Governor his Excellency John Owen MBE. The ship was sunk on 17 September by pumping 8500 gallons of water into the sealed areas from the Cuban ship that had tugged the boat from Cuba to Cayman Brac. Jean Michel Cousteau stayed on board while she sank. It took most of the day to sink. The wreck is now covered with marine life.

South Shore

Sergeant Major Reef – minimum depth 8 m (30 ft); maximum depth 15 m (50 ft). This has many gullies, canyons and swim-throughs.

Orange Canyon – minimum depth 20 m (65 ft); maximum depth 30 m (100 ft). This consists of three large tunnels in the reef.

Pillar Coral Reef – minimum depth 8 m (30 ft); maximum depth 15 m (50 ft). This sonsists of canyons, pillar corals and gullies.

Prince Frederick Wreck – minimum depth 5 m (20 ft); maximum depth 15 m (50 ft). This is the wreck site of a wooden-hulled, twin-masted schooner 33 m (110 ft) long that was both a steam and sailing ship and which was sunk in the late 1800s. The schooner's anchor and chains and its cast iron masts and copper nails have all been retained.

Bluff Wall and Bert Brothers Boulders – minimum depth 20 m (65 ft); maximum depth 30 m (100 ft). This is a steep, vertical wall which is very dramatic.

CENTRAL CARIBBEAN MARINE INSTITUTE

The CCMI (founded in 1998) is an academic and non-profit organisation whose 'mission is to conduct and facilitate research, education and outreach that will sustain marine diversity for future generations'. They offer laboratory and residential facilities at their sustainably built research centre where they run several **Education Programs** for students (14–18 yrs) in Ecology and Conservation which make an excellent introduction to degrees in Marine Biology. They also run **Dive with a Researcher** programs where divers can accompany experts. Check www.reefresearch.org for upcoming courses and the most current information on CCMI.

④ LITTLE CAYMAN

Little Cayman is 74 miles northeast of Grand Cayman and 7 miles from Cayman Brac. It is 10 miles long and one mile wide with a population of 150. It has one grocery store, one bank, one school teacher and hardly any cars. The main form of transport is the bicycle. Little Cayman has the largest colony of red footed booby birds at the 203-acre Booby Pond Nature Reserve. There are iguanas everywhere – their estimated population being 2000 – so more than people. In fact, there is a sign by the airport that says 'iguanas have the right of way'.

The Edward Bodden Airfield consists of a grass landing strip and one wooden shack that also serves as the reception of Paradise Villas which is only yards from the airport.

Blossom Village Square is the main shopping area here you will find the island's only grocery store. The **Hungry Iguana** restaurant is nearby.

Owen Island is described as Cayman's fourth island and used to be connected to Little Cayman. It is a private island with a beautiful white sandy beach. It is so close that you can swim to the island. You can also take a boat or kayak from Kingston Bight or Southern Cross for a picnic or sunbathing.

▲ Male blue iguana

Point of Sand Beach is situated on the eastern tip of the island and has very clear water which is great for snorkelling. Here, you can imagine you are on a truly deserted beach. Drive east along the coast road from the airport to Point o Sand at the very end.

Little Cayman Marine Research Centre is currently being built and will be a Cayman style building with accommodation for students, classrooms, laboratories and a library.

Booby Pond Nature Reserve is a salt water lagoon. From the **National Trust House**, you can use binoculars to spy one of the 20 000 red footed boobies.

Little Cayman Museum is a white, wooden building but smaller than Cayman Brac's. It showcases the shipbuilding and seafaring traditions of the 1850s, including many pirate tales, old photographs, island-made furniture, turtle shells and thatch rope.

The **Baptist Church of Little Cayman** is a modern building next to the original, picturesque, wooden church.

Tarpon Lake is another bird watcher's paradise. Make sure that you also visit the **East End Lighthouse, Snipe Point, Grape Tree, and Jackson's and Spot Bay ponds.** The **Salt Rock Nature Trail** is very unspoilt. **Gladys Howard**, owner of the **Pirates Point Resort**, organises walks.

Near **Sam McCoy's Dive Lodge** is the **Salt Rocks Dock** which is the island's main harbour.

Peter Hilenbrand, the owner of the **Southern Cross Beach Club**, is in the process of becoming the eco-friendly champion for environmental causes above and below the water. The club was rebuilt to eco-friendly standards after Hurricane Ivan. Electricity saving and water and solid waste disposal has been taken into account properly. Guests will have the option of going 'green' by using the basic amenities powered by photovoltaic energy.

GG21 (Green Globe 21) is a certifications programme for eco-friendly resorts and Hillenbrand wants Southern Cross to reach this level. It is a programme based on Agenda 21 which sets out the principles for sustainable development agreed at the UN earth summit at Rio de Janeiro in 1992.

Before Hurricane Ivan, the Department of Tourism had put together an environmental programme to help hotels and attractions in the Cayman Islands reach the levels of Green Globe certification. This was interrupted by Ivan. In the Caribbean there are 57 certified properties, 20 in Jamaica, but none yet in the Cayman Islands.

Hotels, apartments, restaurants and dive, snorkelling and fishing operators

Paradise Villas
Tel: 948 0001
This is a short walk away from the airport.

Southern Cross Club Resort
Tel: 948 1099
This consists of 12 beach villas offering sport fishing, diving and great cuisine.

Little Cayman Beach Resort
Tel: 948 1033
This offers 40 rooms.

Sam McCoy's Dive Lodge
Tel: 948 0026

Pirate's Point Resort
Tel: 948 1010
This is a beachfront resort with a freshwater pool and a great restaurant. Gladys Howard is the owner. She was born in Texas and is a keen diver and chef who has lived on Little Cayman since the 1980s. She organises Sunday morning walks along the **Salt Rock Nature Trail**.

Sir Turtle Beach Villas
Info@sirturtlebeachvillas.com
www.sirturtlebeachvillas.com
These villas offer four bedrooms and two bathrooms in an island style. They are all beachfront villas with fantastic sea views. The area, in South Hole, overlooking the Caribbean Sea, is perfect for bird watchers, scuba divers and snorkellers. The RAMSAR Bird Sanctuary is next door.

Little Cayman Cottage
Tel: 345 945 4144
Penny Cumber reservations@caymanvillas.com
This cottage sits on a white sandy beach with seagrape and palm trees, and is less than one mile from the airport and Blossom Village.

Blossom Village
Tel: 345 945 4144
Penny Cumber reservations@caymanvillas.com
This 100 year-old Caymanian cottage is within walking distance of Blossom Village.

Conch Club Condominiums
Tel: 727 323 8727
www.conchclub.com
These are two and three-bedroom townhouses with an ocean front view. You can use the amenities at the Little Cayman Beach Resort.

Restaurants

Bird of Paradise
Little Cayman Beach Resort
Tel: 948 1033

Kingston Bight
Tel: 948 1015

McCoys
Tel: 948 0026

Pirates Point
Tel: 948 1010

Hungry Iguana
Tel: 948 0007

Southern Cross Club
Tel: 948 1099

Dive, snorkelling and fishing operators

Southern Cross
Tel: 948 1099

Conch Club Divers
Tel: 948 1026

Captain Castro's
Tel: 927 7848

Paradise Divers
Tel: 948 0001

Reef Divers
Tel: 948 1033

DIVING

Little Cayman's Bloody Bay Dive Site has been said to be as spectacular as the Grand Canyon, Amazon Rainforest or the Swiss Alps. This site is 400 yards out from the shore and starts at 20 feet, dropping dramatically to over 6000 feet. Photographs do not do justice to the actual dive – experiencing this is the best thing to do. These are some of the best dives:

North Shore

Black tip tunnels – minimum depth 15 m (50 ft); maximum depth 20 m (65 ft). This consists of caves, swim-throughs and tunnels.

Crystal Palace Wall – minimum depth 18 m (60 ft); maximum depth 30 m (100 ft).

Snapshot – minimum depth 13 m (40 ft); maximum depth 20 m (65 ft).

Magic Roundabout – minimum depth 7m (25 ft); maximum depth 30 m (100 ft). The wall here is vertical and very dramatic. You will find coral heads and huge sponges and a single coral pinnacle on the outer wall.

The Meadows – minimum depth 6m (20 ft); maximum depth 15 m (50 ft). Here in the gullies and canyons you will find garden eels, many silverside minnows, jacks and barracudas.

Eagle Ray Roundup – minimum depth 7m (25 ft); maximum depth 14 m (45 ft). Here you will see eagle rays, jacks and stingrays swimming in an amphitheatre. Sometimes you may see a 3 m (10 ft) manta ray known as Molly.

Three Fathom Wall – minimum depth 5.5 m (20 ft); maximum depth 30 m (100 ft). This has many swim-throughs.

Marilyns' Cut – This has a very deep, sheer wall and is known for its barrel and rope sponges. You will also find large barracuda.

Great Wall West and Sheer Wall – minimum depth 10 m (35 ft); maximum depth 30 m (100 ft). This is a completely flat, vertical wall.

South Shore

Grundy's Gardens – minimum depth 20 m (65 ft); maximum depth 30 m (100 ft). This site, named after Mike Grundy of the Cayman Island's Marine Conservation Unit, consists of many coral columns.

Soto Trader – minimum depth 20 m (65 ft); maximum depth 30 m (100 ft). This was a boat 36 m (120 ft) long by 9 m (30 ft) wide which caught fire and sank in April 1975.

Bibliography

Cathy Church, *My Underwater Photo Journey*

Michael Craton and the New History Committee, *Founded upon the Seas A History of the Cayman Islands and their People*, Ian Randle Publishers

Courtney Platt and Joanna Lawrence, *Paradise Interrupted Hurricane Ivan 11–12 September 2004*

Stephan Talty, *Empire of Blue Water*, Crown Publishers, New York

Martha Hodes, *The Sea Captain's Wife*, W W Norton, New York

Roger C Smith, *The Maritime Heritage of the Cayman Islands*, University Press of Florida